REMOVE TROUBLE FROM YOUR HEART

Esther Pasztory

EAST EUROPEAN MONOGRAPHS, BOULDER, COLORADO
DISTRIBUTED BY COLUMBIA UNIVERSITY PRESS, NEW YORK
2008

EAST EUROPEAN MONOGRAPHS, NO. DCCXXIX

ISBN: 978-0-88033-627-7

Library of Congress Control Number: 2008930294

Printed in the United States of America

Newspaper photograph of the groups of refugees that came to the US in December 1956. Woods Hole, Cape Cod.

From left to right: Klara Miskolczy, Kristina Miskolczy, Ferenc Borbiro, Esther Miskolczy, László Miskolczy, and Babszi Bodroghy

For Richard

Contents

Acknowledgments

I would like to thank Andrew Finegold for help with the illustrations and Edee Howland for help in proofreading.

Dear Reader:

This is a memoir of a refugee who came to the US as a teenager after the collapse of the 1956 anti-communist revolution in Hungary. 2006 is the fiftieth anniversary of the revolution and a time to take stock of the human cost that the drastic difference between Hungary and the US created in many. This story chronicles the difficulty of belonging to two cultures at the same time on both the personal and professional level which sometimes means too many of two good things. The author's solution of escaping to a third ancient culture for a life work allows for a fantasy world where the spirit is free to roam. The realm of the Aztec and Inca, America's great Antiquity, is interwoven with the loves and vicissitudes of a Hungarian-American searching for identity and a feeling of roots. It is a story many people with a dual heritage can understand and the more securely placed can imagine. In fact, this book is a positive step in the process of coming to terms with multiple identities.

The Author

Memory 1956
Help. Help. Help. SOS. SOS. SOS.

I will never forget November 4, 1956. I woke up at dawn to deafening noises that I took to be fireworks celebrating the success of the previous days' revolution. I was thirteen and my sister in the other bed in the room was eleven. I lay in bed listening contentedly watching the light flash through the shutters after all the excitement that went before. Then my parents rushed into the room, since we had the only radio, and turned it on. The euphoria was short-lived. The Russians were shelling the city, tanks were rolling on the street and the revolution was over. The revolutionary Prime Minister, Imre Nagy, was on the radio shortly. Nagy's voice shook with restrained emotion as he informed the public that the Russians had attacked Budapest that morning, that the Hungarian government and the troops would do everything to defend the country and that he was thus informing the rest of the world as to what happened, implying that he hoped for help. The announcement was short, bleak, and deadly serious. Then they played the national anthem with its sad words of defeat and survival and sonorous music written in 1848 when the revolution of independence against Austria was put down by the Russian army. Then there was quiet on the radio and someone put on Beethoven's Seventh Symphony which was perhaps lying about the studio and that was played over and over in its serious and powerful harmonies all day long. It was more moving than any words would have been. I sat quietly by the radio crying.

About seven in the morning someone announced on the radio that the UN Security Council was going to discuss the situation in Hungary. Everyone was elated. Radio Free Europe had been encouraging anti-soviet activities in the Iron Curtain countries for years with the implication that the West in general and the US in particular would help when necessary. It was now necessary and there was infinite hope that the West would come across.

By eight AM however nothing more happened than the Russian ultimatum that if the insurgency did not end they would bomb the city from the air. (Which luckily they never did.) I learned later that in the evening the Vienna Associated Press office got a telex message from the Hungarian Writers' Association to please tell the world what is happening in Hungary, saying the radio was still in the insurgents' hands and ended with "Help, Help, Help, SOS, SOS, SOS." But the West did not come then or later; they remained silent.

Then about 8 PM Beethoven stopped playing and the station went blank. The Russians had taken over the radio and there were no more revolutionary broadcasts. We spent the day glued to the radio, unable to believe that all was over. We went out on the terrace and watched the Russian tanks like giant caterpillars drive up and down the hill road. Buda, where we were living, was in the suburban hills part of Budapest, a city divided in two by the Danube. In Buda we were far from the actual fighting which was mostly in Pest. We could hear the artillery, see the tanks, but we were relatively safe. There was nothing to do.

Sporadic gunfire continued for days and even weeks after November 4, but basically it was all over in one day. The Russians and Communism were back to stay. I would have to go on studying the declension of Russian words which I hated. The "normalcy" of communism would return. Imre Nagy and whomever they could get ahold of were found and eventually executed. It is said that Eisenhower did not help Hungary for fear of unleashing a war with Russia, sort of a Third World War. Maybe he was right, maybe he was not. We will never know. But Hungarians who had tended to idolize the West were deeply embittered by this abandonment.

The revolution had started ten days earlier on October 23, when a demonstration unexpectedly took over the radio station and began broadcasting anti-communist incitements. It was spontaneously joined by students, factory workers, inhabitants of Budapest and by people all over the country. The country had had enough of the Russian regime and simply erupted. One of their immediate aims was purely symbolic – toppling the colossal bronze Stalin statue which required professional welders to accomplish. Only his boots remained and on the photos one can see that they were as tall as two people, one on top of the other. Having vented this rage on the statue, the populace, in organizational meetings, announced the demands of the revolution – the hated Russian puppet leader Mátyás Rákosi, the butt of jokes with his bald head, was to be removed, and Imre Nagy was to take his place. Imre Nagy was still a communist – Hungarians did not imagine that they could get away without a communist – but he was closest in spirit to the revolution and the desire for freedom from Russia and totalitarian rule. The aim of the revolution was to get rid of the Russians occupying the country since 1945 and of their communist puppets. All this coalesced in the demand for Imre Nagy as Prime Minister.

On the morning of the 24th of October, the telephone kept ringing with my classmates' mothers full of rumors about an uprising the night before. My mother did not let us go to school and the day before was the last I ever went. It then seemed like a welcome day of vacation. My father was not in town; he was at the vineyard overseeing the harvest and knew nothing about the revolution for days. There were rumors that boys as young as fourteen and eleven were joining the insurgents and though we were girls my mother was very concerned that we should not go out of the house and get killed. She made us solemnly swear that we would not go out of the house or if we did, for some reason, we would not speak to anyone. She was afraid of our idealism. There was nothing for it but to sit by the radio and listen to the bulletins, all of which were encouraging. The bulletins were interspersed with music. The heroism of the young boys was awe-inspiring, perhaps some of my classmates were involved; I didn't know. It was hard to sit by the radio all day. The rebellion was succeeding even to the point that Imre Nagy formed a provisional government. While at first no one believed in its success, the days passed and it seemed to be succeeding, and people started believing. Hundreds of nameless individuals cut the communist emblem out of the red, white, and green Hungarian flag, and flags with holes hung from windows all over Budapest. There were Russian tanks but they hadn't mounted a major counteroffensive, and there were also Molotov cocktails to take care of them. For almost ten days there was the heady scent of success. Hungarians claimed that the Russians rarely got out of their tanks due to a supposed order keeping them in there so the soldiers would not see how much higher the standard of living was even in communist Hungary than in Russia and foment a rebellion of their own. Poems were written, jokes were passed around among the freedom fighters. After it was all over these were carefully kept in hiding places as sacred relics.

After a few days of staying in the house we had to go out to get provisions such as milk, eggs, bread, flour. There were immediate shortages in the stores everywhere and I remember standing in endless lines buying whatever was available under the watchful eyes of patrolling tanks. It seemed to my thirteen-year-old self that revolutions consisted of standing in line for victuals. In the lines people talked. They talked about acts of heroism witnessed by someone, about children running away from home, about what the Americans would or would not do. My father arrived a few days later. His car was full of fruit – apples, grapes, pears, country fare – and he came through where the action was in Pest, finally seeing for himself the truth of the rumors of a successful rebellion. He gave most of his food to the freedom fighters who were eager to have it since food was getting scarce. He arrived full of excitement, telling of first-hand contacts with the freedom fighters. My mother was very glad to see him back in this crisis. I don't know all the things my father did in the subsequent days except that he went to his office and gave everyone, including himself, the secret information the communists kept on them. These were sort of "reliability cards" kept locked up for communist eyes only. His own card read: "Upper middle class background and entirely unreliable."

For the first few days of November as nothing happened either from the Russians or from the West, we all settled down to believing that the rebellion was miraculously successful, that Hungary got out from under the Russian yoke and life would be better. In this my father was as naïve as anyone else. We children were elated by excitement and visions of a new world which of course we could not even imagine. No one could sleep well and we did nothing restlessly during the day.

One of the first things the revolutionaries did was to open the borders so people could go freely to "the West." Some people did not wait to find out how the revolution would turn out but collected their valuables and took trains, cars, carts out of the country immediately. I don't know when my father started to think about it because this topic was not discussed with us children. However, I am sure that it was days after November 4 since my parents believed in the success of the revolution until then. In the next ten days there were many comings and goings and secret discussions between my parents from which we were excluded and we wondered what was happening. Sometime around the fifteenth of

November we were told that my mother's nerves were acting up from all this excitement and we had to go visit some relatives in the country where it was quiet. We were to visit Babszi, my aunt Marta's sister in Keszthely. We were also to wear two sets of our oldest and grubbiest clothes, which in our case meant pleated skirts and sweaters, because we were not to carry luggage. We just had little handbags. As the weather was freezing cold, we needed overcoats and winter gear. Thus bundled up we set out one morning, it could have been on foot or by taxi, I don't remember, but in any case, we left the precious car in the garage, locked the door, left all of our belongings, including the cat, and set off towards the Southern Railway Station which wasn't terribly far.

At this point general chaos reigned in the city. At the railway station there were some trains on the tracks, but no schedules, tickets or visible railway agents. We got into a car not knowing fully where it was going, but from that station trains generally went west. The cars were full of people staring sternly ahead and not wanting to say a word to anyone. We sat in total and uncomfortable silence pretending that all was normal. Were they all going for a few days vacation to soothe their nerves? After a few hours the train began to move and it went a certain distance. Then it stopped and we got out with all the rest of the people waiting on the platform to see if some other train would come. Eventually another unscheduled train showed up and by taking three or more trains some unspecified distances, we arrived in Keszthely. We had been to Keszthely before some summer; it is a nice little town on Lake Balaton, and we knew my aunt Babszi well since she often visited in Budapest. When she did, she showed pictures of her sons Thomas and Balint who had all successfully snuck out of the country years before and were now in Australia and Canada. She would tease me and say that I would one day marry one of them. She lived in Keszthely with her father, a very distinguished looking man of eighty I hardly knew. Keszthely was a place where my mother could have found peace and quiet away from the crushed revolution in Budapest. However, here too there were lots of secret discussions among the grownups to which we were not privy, and a few days later it was announced that we would go on to visit yet another relative, never heard of, who lived much further west near the Austrian border.

It did not require great genius from a thirteen-year-old to figure out that we were leaving the country just like all those people on the trains. My sister and I confronted our parents with this interpretation and they finally told the truth. My father claimed that he did not tell us for our own good – had the Russians beaten us up we would have blurted out the truth and we would have all been killed. Leaving the country was a crime punishable by death. Not telling us meant, however, that we did not have a chance to say goodbye to our favorite dolls, to our cat, nor could we take some little memento with us. We never said goodbye to our friends and classmates, most of whom we never saw again. We left to go to the country for a few days and never came back.

With some more irregular trains we went to a little village, whose name I discovered only in the last ten years, Csepreg, which I then thought was some kind of a farmstead but was in fact the house of relative of Babszi. Babszi and her father came with us apparently planning to leave the country together. In all likelihood it may been Babszi's intense desire to go that pushed my father over the line in making the decision. By the time we got to Csepreg it was November 20 or so, and the communist government was reestablishing the border. It was not yet an "iron curtain," but one could no longer walk across in broad daylight with all one's possessions. The border had to be crossed at night and local young men acted as guides to be paid in wristwatches and jewelry. One could no longer set out alone, one needed serious help. Russian tanks were already active in the area. My father found some local young men who suggested that a good way of crossing the border was by lying on the bottom of a hay cart with hay piled on top making us invisible. Such a scheme was generally agreed to for the following day.

The next day the young men arrived quite shaken up. They had done the hay ride with some other people the night before but the Russians got wind of it and shot into the carts, killing those persons. If we wanted to go we would have to walk. Was the eighty-year-old gentleman capable of nine kilometers on rough terrain? He insisted he was, probably thinking what did he have to lose, he wanted to see his other daughter once more in Woods Hole, Massachusetts, USA. Then the young men examined us saying we had to get rid of all bags and possessions and go just with our clothes on our backs. My mother had a small bag she was very reluctant to give up. "What's in the bag?" asked the young men laughing and opened the zipper – it was full of chocolate bars and soap. Blushing, my mother explained that this was in case we were made prisoners; the soap was to keep us clean and the chocolate bars were quick energy. Everyone laughed. Of course if they made prisoners of us we would be shot on the spot. In the end everything was removed and we waited for late at night to set off.

We were to walk arm in arm or hand in hand. My sister and I, my mother and father, and Babszi and her father. There was a cloudy sky with the moon occasionally visible as through a transparent curtain. Most of the time it was completely dark. The temperature was at or near freezing. Generally, we were walking over newly plowed fields that had frozen rock solid. The furrows were over a foot deep and irregular, so that at every step you fell or were likely to fall into the next one. The rhythm was step–fall–pick yourself up, step–fall–pick yourself up. My sister and I held onto each other as we bobbed up and down without rhyme or rhythm, gritting our teeth. All talking was forbidden and we walked in complete silence. Between concentrating on the furrows and being afraid of the Russians we sometimes thought of all our known world that was receding and of the unknown we were going towards. It was a very strange excitement.

At one point we had to cross a bridge over a river patrolled by tanks and were suddenly motioned to fall into a ditch by a guide so as not to be seen by the Russian searchlights patrolling every inch of the area. There was a rumbling in the distance. We could hear the tank approaching closer, the searchlight swiveling in every direction. My heart was pounding and I was holding my breath. One false move from any one of us and we would be dead. I remember involuntarily raising my head at one point and one of the young men yanking me down to earth by my ponytail very hard. They passed around a flask of brandy as everyone lay there shivering in the ditch. There were several more hours of frozen furrows to cross, numb with cold and fear, but luckily there were no other encounters with Russians. The border itself was not marked by anything except a very shallow ditch easy to overlook. When we were on the other side the guides collected the wristwatches and we thanked them. They were doing this in the spirit of the revolution, not merely for gain, and their lives were at risk every night. By December crossing the border became very difficult. But in that short time two hundred thousand people left Hungary.

We crossed the border on November 24 and followed the lights the guides pointed out to Austria. The Austrians were very kind. We woke up someone at 2 AM and were eventually put in a church with other refugees. Through the help of private individuals and local charities we managed to get to Vienna in a few days. My father had contacts there and evidently someone owed him enough money so we could stay in a cheap hotel for about a week. We had no clothes except what we were wearing – the local charities gave us something clean.

We had to go to Vienna to register as refugees and to look for a host country. We were fingerprinted, questioned and investigated. After all, we could have been spies. They were investigating by cross-examining other refugees as to whether we told the truth about who we were, what our characters were. Hungary is a small country, a lot of people knew each other – it was amazing how quickly the truth came out. They asked nothing of us girls.

Vienna was full of Hungarian refugees and my parents ran into several friends. "You left, too!" "Yes, you left, too!" Various countries had representatives accepting refugees and people moved excitedly from one to the other. Where should they go? My father had two possible destinations in mind – Brussels in Belgium and Sao Paolo in Brazil – since in both he had architect friends who could help him get a job. He spoke French which made Belgium more practical, but probably he could learn Portuguese. But the real surprise in Vienna was that the US, which had hitherto only a tiny quota for Hungarians, opened its doors to let in a great number. (Previously Babszi's sons had to go to Australia and Canada because the US did not allow them in.) This generosity was perhaps in compensation for not actually aiding the revolution, but nevertheless it was much appreciated. The choice was dizzying. My father never considered going to the US before but now he considered it. The reason for it was family – what family we had abroad was in the US. There was the much hated Marta who left my father's brother for Albert Szent-Györgyi, who had received the Nobel Prize, and her two children my cousins Gabor and Orsi who were now grown. With us was Babszi, Marta's sister. Shouldn't the family be all together even if it's the US? He talked to Marta on the telephone and she was eager that we should come; she emphasized the opportunities and she couldn't wait to see her sister and father. And maybe for my father this was the biggest adventure of them all. For a while all was in flux. Where will we feel most at home – Europe, North or South America? What language should we speak – French, Portuguese or English? We children were never asked our opinion just as we were never asked whether we wanted to leave Hungary in the first place. My father signed us all up for the US.

Having chosen the US my father geared up for action. None of us spoke a word of English so he bought a German-English language book and held English classes in the hotel room every day. He claimed that during the First World War he met some English sailors on the Danube in Baja who taught him a few phrases. The first lesson in the book suggested learning a specific sentence, which has become unforgettable to me: "The early bird catches the worm." What was the author thinking of? My father pronounced it sort of in the Queen's English as "Da arly bard katches da varm." We had to unlearn all these memorized sayings in the US.

Thinking that this was some kind of cultural tour, my father dragged us through all kinds of museums in Vienna where he particularly wanted us to see his favorite Brueghel paintings, which I remember only as a blur of little figures. This was the West with its fabled arts that he had not been allowed to see all these years. Somehow our minds were not on paintings. My mother wanted to see the movie "Gone With The Wind" which was then playing in the movie theaters. The book was forbidden by the communists because they thought the conflict between the Confederacy and the Union in the US might spark a civil war in Hungary. My mother probably wanted to see Vivian Leigh. But in the scenes of the burning of Atlanta she got hysterical and we all started crying because it was too reminiscent of the shelling of Budapest and so we had to leave the movie theater without seeing the end. The normalcy my father required of us was sometimes too much.

Once we got on the US list at a certain point we had to go to a camp and wait there to be assigned means of travel. Our camp near Wiener Neustadt was probably as good as refugee camps go, with overcrowded beds, epidemics of diarrhea and unclean toilets, and the two weeks seemed like an eternity. We were then moved to another camp near the airport until finally we were on the airplane crossing the Atlantic. For us children this crossing has remained memorably awful. None of the Hungarians on the plane had ever been in an airplane, including us. The plane was an old four-engined propeller plane, two of whose engines stopped functioning halfway across the Atlantic. We had to stop twice, in Shannon and Gander, to refuel. There was not only plenty of turbulence, there was a storm across the Atlantic. People sighed, moaned, and screamed most of the way "Oh my God, Oh my God" (*Istenem, Istenem*). We also, pretty much all, threw up the whole time convulsively. The stewardesses vainly tried to serve coffee, it kept spilling all over. I remember that flight as smelling of coffee, oranges and vomit. However, we made it to Camp Kilmer in New Jersey.

In retrospect that nightmarish journey expressed everyone's state of mind. We were all devastated by the collapse of the revolution, by having left home in the hands of ruthless communists and though we were alive, ahead of us was an unknown deeper than the Atlantic we were so afraid of falling into with the wobbly plane. We felt guilty that we were leaving our homeland. We had no idea what lay ahead, what monsters had to be battled, what pains to be endured or even what joys were to be found, but we were going to somewhere strange and foreign and who is to say that we would be at home there? It wasn't just my mother whose nerves were acting up; everyone's nerves were on the very edge. So we vomited and screamed throughout the crossing.

Camp Kilmer was wonderful. A military unit used for civilian purposes, it was large, bright, and clean with plenty of room for bunk beds for families. The most amazing was the dining room where big blacks with broad smiles ladled out large servings of meats, potatoes, vegetables, cakes and jello on metal trays with compartments for each, with as many seconds as you wanted. People went back to their bunks with oranges, bananas, and apples but were too full to eat them before the next gargantuan meal. Megaphones asked people not to take food back since it was rotting on the windowsills and they would get enough the next meal. The refugees, however, were not used to this and continued hoarding food. There was also a supply room in which there were huge piles of new clothes – mostly sturdy army socks and underwear. One could take as much as one wanted. We had been wearing our clothes for a month and fresh underwear was great.

Marta's son Gabor came to fetch us in a few days with a station wagon big enough for all seven of us. A young physicist, he was our first introduction to America outside the camp. The trip to me was something from science fiction. I was amazed by the four-lane highways with the double yellow lines in the middle that sometimes parted for beautifully manicured islands of grass and trees. Much of the highways seemed like a beautiful park. I was also astonished by all the overpasses and underpasses and complicated roads that seemed like something out of the novels of H. G. Wells. I hadn't moved geographically from one place to another, I had moved in time from the past to the future. And these incredible roads were full of large colorful cars, not at all like the little black car we left in the garage in Budapest. The first letter I would write to my friend Edda was all about these roads.

I could observe it all because there was not much conversation in the car. Everyone was exhausted and bewildered. Occasionally my cousin asked the group if they wanted to stop at Howard Johnson's where they had twenty-seven flavors of ice cream, but we all said "no" politely, because in Hungary people don't eat ice cream in the winter for fear of getting a sore throat. We thought cousin Gabor, or perhaps America, was demented. This difference in customs was to be the very tip of the iceberg.

We arrived in Woods Hole the week of Christmas. The Szent-Györgi's had a large white wooden house with many rooms. Surprise number two – wooden houses. We were used to brick or concrete. They had the first television I ever saw and I was surprised by the advertising which seemed unnatural to me. Aunt Marta took us shopping for American style clothes. She told us to practice smiling because in America everybody smiles. We practiced smiling in front of mirrors. People came to the house caroling. They were followed by reporters heralding our arrival in the local newspapers; these were followed by photographers recording the arrival of refugees in pictures. In the most ambitious one of them all, my father and I stand in the center radiating cheer and optimism. I am wearing my new Sunday best blouse and skirt (I now had six more blouses for everyday wear), my sister wears Marta's Fair Isle sweater but with her pigtails she looks like an exotic country girl. Babszi seems straight from the kitchen already with apron and potholder, her father looking equally at home in a bathrobe. My mother on the far left looks ill and exhausted with circles under her eyes. Everybody is trying to give a little smile.

Marta was an organizational genius. With a family friend named Clara Mayer who was influential, she arranged that Kristina and I should go to boarding schools and found fellowships for me at the Cambridge School of Weston where her daughter Orsi had gone and for Kristina at the Windsor Mountain School. By January when the Spring semester began, we and our new blouses were taken to those schools. She also suggested that my parents go to New York where the architectural firms were and arranged for a contact with the firm of Harrison and Abramowitz. She thought such separations were necessary so we could learn English quickly and find ourselves appropriate places in the American world. After we had been thus established, what with geographic distance, subsequent closeness with Marta and her family was a rare occasion and not an everyday reality as my father had imagined. The family wasn't really united in the US. That was true with us, too. Except for vacation, after Woods Hole, our family never lived all together again.

1
Self-Made Man

"There are no old jokes; to a newborn all jokes are new."

My father was the most capable man I have ever known. He could do everything that required manual dexterity such as fixing things around the house. He could ice-skate elegantly with his hands behind his back. He could row a fishing dinghy on the Danube near his hometown of Baja or row races with the exclusive rowing clubs of Budapest. He learned to ski in the Alps and taught me how to go downhill as well as uphill in the absence of a lift (which I hated). He danced with a natural rhythm and I learned the Viennese waltz and the Continental tango from him. In his wild youth, which was a legend, he raced cars with a friend in Switzerland, Bruno Walter. My sister still has the trophy, a silver tray whose design traces their route on a winning trip. He could also dismember half a pig in the Budapest bathtub, cutting up chops and ribs and filling casings with spicy sausage meat for the larder. His bedtime stories for me came from physics and astronomy. I remember one in particular that I now know as the Big Bang Theory of the origin of the universe. He claimed to be able to play the flute, although he didn't have a flute in my childhood and I never heard him play, but I never doubted it. He mainly liked modern music which to him meant Wagner. He liked everything modern in clothes, architecture, furnishings.

And yet in many ways he was a nineteenth century person in his values and customs. He kissed ladies on the hand even in America. He told stories of how he had even fought a duel in his youth. The provocation was apparently trivial. He was challenged by an aristocratic party and could not say no except by humiliating himself. Having no experience dueling, he went to a weapons expert who recommended the broadsword as the easiest weapon and gave him a few lessons. His advice was "keep hitting the guy on the head." There was no serious consequence to this duel; the amazing thing is that it was fought at all in the early twentieth century.

My father was born in 1900 in the mid-size town of Baja that is now near the southern border of Hungary. The Danube is very wide there but a smaller arm of it came to the very center of Baja. One could swim, boat, and ice-skate there. In 1900 Baja was a sleepy agricultural town. If you asked my father or uncle who their ancestors were, they usually said with a chuckle that they came from a long line of peasants and did not search into the matter. My father was the last of four boys born to Ilona (Helen) Nagy Czirok and my grandfather Ferenc (Francis) Miskolczy. Their parents lived in the country outside Baja in Bácska province and were farmers. My cousin Gabor has done genealogical researches but couldn't trace the name much beyond the eighteenth century. That makes perfect sense in that it was in 1686 that the Austrians chased the Turks out of Hungary and settled life with baptismal records resumed. The Turks occupied Hungary for about two hundred years and in that time a certain chaos reigned in the country. Only a few, especially aristocratic, families can trace their histories past the Turkish era of occupation. Moreover, in the old days spellings were variable and the name could be spelled Miskoczi of Miskolci in any kind of combination. Peoples also took up new Hungarian-sounding names if they belonged to other ethnic groups if it was to their advantage or desire. Various other families with the Miskolczy name exist now in Hungary whose relationship to one another is nil or unclear. My mother often called my father "a peasant' when she wanted to insult him, an appellation which he acknowledged cheerfully.

My grandfather was the first in the family to have enough learning to become town clerk and move into Baja where his sons were born. I remember him as a very stern old man I tried to stay away from during my summer holidays in Baja. My father told of severe beatings from him, and I wasn't going to risk any. Evidently my father was a very mischievous and risk-taking child whose exploits included going out on thin ice and nearly drowning and overturning my grandfather's precious beehives. Bee-keeping was my grandfather's passion.

My grandmother died in her thirties from a burst appendix and the lack of decent medical care in Baja during the First World War. Little is known about her except that she was a very loving woman. No photos survive. My father was her last child and he was a teenager when she died. His name was László (Ladislaus) nicknamed Laci. She hoped very much that my father would be a girl and dressed him in girl's clothes when he was little. Later on she hoped that he would become a priest. But there was no question of that.

The family acquired the nickname of "storks" because they were so tall. Over six feet, my father was much taller than the average Hungarian. Of the other tall brothers, Sándor (Alexander) died during the First World War in the military. Everyone considered him to have been the smartest of the brothers. The oldest, Dezső (Desiderius), became a doctor famous in Eastern Europe specializing in neurology. He lived much of his life in Transylvania (Romania). Ferenc (Francis) became an artist, spending time in Germany and Spain, but settling in the hometown of Baja. He was considered a ne'er-do-well. My father bought him a charming modern, Bauhaus style house with a turret by the Danube which came to be called Owl Castle. Uncle Feri specialized in watercolors of views of the Danube and many of his works are in the Baja museum. I and other members of the family have quite a few as well. The family generally looked down on Feri's art as too old-fashioned and saccharine and he never made it in a major art center such as Budapest. But he was a success in Baja, took care of his father and stepmother and of the family plot in the cemetery which he always made us visit when we were there. He lived to be the oldest and died a decorated citizen of Baja at the age of ninety. He left Owl Castle to the town.

My father was drafted at the age of eighteen and saw action in Italy. Luckily the war was soon over and he entered the Polytechnic University (Műegyetem) in Budapest to become an architect. He never said much about that experience and it is assumed that he did well. He was a young man in a hurry. He wanted to build significant things, he wanted to make money, and he wanted to enjoy the good life. He married only at age forty-two and often said that he wouldn't marry until he had a million (I guess in Hungarian currency). He did not want to be a penny-pincher and live in poverty like his ancestors.

In the 1920's and 30's he designed private houses, apartment buildings and factories and teamed up with important entrepreneurs. His best known building was a resort hotel in the mountains of northern Hungary called Kékes. When it was built in 1935 it was in avant-garde Bauhaus style, a flat roofed rectangular building with no frills except for a lot of windows. Like Frank Lloyd Wright, my father believed in using local materials and local stone was used for the outer walls and fireplace and flooring. Photos of the hotel were featured in German architectural magazines. When it was built this hotel was the last word in luxury. After the communist takeover it was turned into a sanatorium and began a long process of decay. When I saw it in the 1990's Kékes was a depressing sight with a hole where the swimming pool used to be and grimy stones where guests once read the newspaper and had coffee on the patio. I was most impressed by the circular dining room and the general geometric layout which seemed like my father's style. But 1920's luxury was evidently quite modest – the rooms were small. It was quite clear to me that the hotel could no longer be rehabilitated as a hotel without major rebuilding. I had never seen the Kékes of my childhood, but I saw pictures of my father standing in front of it proudly wearing the then-fashionable knickers or with his red convertible.

I don't know if he made a "million" but he seemed to be a wealthy man and he saw himself as a wealthy man. After the collapse of communism the government made it possible to claim via vouchers property and goods confiscated by the communists and we looked into my father's property. Surprisingly, it turned out that my father had few tangible goods that could be discovered through some records. He had no investment shares, he had had only small pieces of real estate and he didn't have his own house. We lived in a large three-story villa for free because he had made a deal with the owners to finish an unfinished building. Evidently he bartered in this fashion and made deals and lived like a king but had no substantial fortune. He lived on his cleverness. In the 1950's he collected money someone owed him abroad and bought a car, another private transaction. But a fortune that he could prove he did not have. My father lived in the present.

At various Hungarian parties I would meet an elderly lady who was astonished that I was the daughter of Laci Miskolczy.

"Are you really the daughter of *the* Laci Miskolczy?"

"Yes."

"You mean he actually married????"

"Yes."

"None of us ever thought he'd marry. I could tell you STORIES…."

In fact they never told stories, they merely rolled their eyes, laughed, clapped their hands as if they were reminiscing about something very exciting. My father was apparently a ladies' man and a Don Juan and when accused of wild days in his bachelor life, he merely smiled sheepishly. He never talked about those times or those women. Did he have a mad passionate love affair with anyone? He didn't say. When he married he was totally faithful and turned over a new leaf. However my mother recounted that when she met him he had had a girlfriend and she had to "get rid of her." There were no photos of individual women among his papers, although there were photos of carousing. My father in a tux with a chamber pot on his head, laughing with drinking boon companions, was one. I suppose he was a playboy of sorts.

But like a good son he went home regularly and put in the first bathroom with a flush toilet in his father's house in Baja. My father was a modernizer who believed in progress and civilization. He believed in free enterprise, capitalism, and was a member of the Smallholders Party, a relatively conservative group. He was a handsome man: tall, muscular, a genial face. Like all the Miskolczy men he was partially bald. He loved parties and people and he tended to dominate a room which most people did not mind. He was an inveterate joke-teller and had a repertoire of hundreds of anecdotes. Many he stored in his memory and some he got from joke books he collected. Those of us in the family heard them repeated endless times. If we complained, he always said, "There are no old jokes; to a newborn every joke is new." I have never been able to remember jokes for long though sometimes I tried. He had political jokes, off-color jokes, childish jokes – any kind of jokes. Here is one of his favorites which I do happen to remember:

> A gentleman sits next to a beautiful lady at a dinner party and leans over and says, 'Will you sleep with me for a penny?' The lady is outraged. 'What do you think I am, sir, to do such a thing!!!' The gentleman says then: 'will you sleep with me for a million dollars?' the lady hesitates a second. The gentleman says quickly, 'We now know what you are, we're just haggling over the price.'

This joke probably goes back to the Egyptians and perhaps beyond. I have come across it here and there in books and movies. My father told it as if it had just been invented and was greatly amused.

During the Second World War my father used all his practical and organizational skills to keep the family, friends, and community alive. In 1940 the dictator Horthy allowed Hungary within Hitler's sphere of influence despite general misgivings. One reason was that Hitler could have squashed Hungary as he did Poland which was perhaps a worse prospect. But another was that Hungary had a great feeling of injustice stemming from the First World War when, allied with the losing powers, she lost two-thirds of her territory to Slovakia, Romania, and Yugoslavia. Referred to as the Treaty of Versailles or the Treaty of Trianon (after the actual place where it was signed), this had been a shame and misery to Hungarians, to say nothing of the fact that a great many families and communities had become separated. Small Hungary was then called, as it still is often, "Crippled Hungary." Hitler promised Hungary that in the event of a victory they could have these areas back and for about a year they did. Some Hungarian politicians like Count Pál Teleki tried to create a situation in which Hungary would be in a special position not quite an ally of Germany. The military was on the German side and when they began to occupy the country Teleki shot himself in protest. Many Hungarians admire that brave action but the end result was that Hungary came under German occupation and Jews were being taken to concentration camps. Eventually the Russian army came to "liberate" Hungary with a decisive siege of the city of Budapest itself which ended in 1945. The siege lasted almost a year and anyone who could either escaped the city or hunkered down in cellars. My father was busy finding adequate cellars for family and for a great many Jews, often his closest friends. Food and water were a problem, dead horses found on the streets were eaten and my mother remembers baking bread for dozens. The streets were full of corpses. Some people found the cellars too claustrophobic and moved up to the apartments during "safe" times only to be bombed to bits. I was about one year old during all this turmoil. There is no doubt in my mind that we survived because of my father's ability to deal with any difficulty. My parents were then young marrieds, my mother twenty-five and pregnant, my father forty-four in fact but twenty-five in spirit. Terrible as those times were to them, they were also a great adventure ultimately successfully completed: they survived. A few weeks after peace was declared my mother gave birth to my sister in a windowless building. Next to the horrific stories that they later told of the war they also conveyed a spirit of unbounded optimism. They could survive anything, surely this had to have been the worst. But it wasn't.

After the war, however, came further humiliation and political instability. The Russian forces never really retreated from Hungary and set up puppet governments. Hungary was under Russian occupation. By 1948 a great many people saw that a totalitarian government was being formed that would be extremely inimical to the upper classes – the old aristocracy, the wealthy businessmen and entrepreneurs, the whole professional class and the educated middle class. This realization was gradual and at first communist rule was not completely consolidated. Seeing these directions though, a great many people left the country taking their wealth and/or possessions with them if possible. Many were the wealthy, but there were many others who didn't have money only skills. My father's favorite writer, Sándor Márai, left in disgust at the corrupt government and lack of freedom and tried to find a home in the US or in Western Europe writing Hungarian novels all the while mostly for expatriates. My father was familiar with many countries on the continent, had friends there, and spoke excellent French and German. Artistic and entrepreneurial in spirit, he considered going too. My mother did not want to go because her parents were living in Transylvania, which had then become a part of Romania, and she wanted to see them before going into exile. All this took so long to be decided between them that in the end she could no longer go to Romania to visit her parents, and the borders to the West were so closed that one could no longer leave the country at all except with great danger to life. From that time until the 1956 revolution, Hungarians could not leave Hungary without risking their life. People tried, and some young men like my second cousin Bálint Bodroghy succeeded. But it was not for a man with a wife and two small daughters.

Having made himself a name as a modern architect, having made some money, and having recently married, my father ended up staying in Hungary and having to find a living and a survival in the communist era. Nothing much remained of the money or of his arrangements but he still had a reputation and expertise – he could build. According to the communist ideology, the future intellectuals were to come from the peasantry and the proletariat and they gave those children advantages in the schools and made the aristocrats and their children work in the fields and factories. Some of my classmates who came from inappropriate families could not go to the university and become doctors and engineers; they were to be nurses and superintendents at best. The fact was, however, that there were as yet no peasant-doctors and peasant-engineers and if all life were not to grind to a halt the old professionals had to be put back into position. Basically all the doctors were back to work and so was my father. He became the head of the City Planning Bureau and planned cities. He became an expert in the reinforced concrete used in low-income housing in which he made innovations. He had, in effect, a whole other second career in which he did quite well. He was recognized for this by the Kossuth award in 1955. The Kossuth Prize was the highest honor Hungary could give.

How did my father deal with this in his own mind? He was not one to talk about such things, but his stories gave indications. One I remember concerned a directive from the ministry that henceforth they design apartment buildings with only shared bathrooms as was then done in Moscow and had been done earlier in Europe. It was too expensive to build a bathroom in each apartment said the minister. My father considered shared bathrooms barbaric in the 1950's and claims to have responded: "Let me see the figures for the Moscow-style apartments and I will prove 'with figures' that I can build cheaper housing with bathrooms in the individual apartments," and he did. His attitude was that he was not going to allow Hungary to sink into barbarism. He seemed to see his role as a civilizing influence.

My best friend's stepfather who was a Count, was kept on by the communists as a master of etiquette for state functions. Since the communist leadership did not know which fork to use and what to wear to international gatherings, he was the authority on all such matters and made a living from it. In one instance I remember from my childhood, my father had a somewhat similar role. In about 1953, when practically no one left the country, my father was asked to accompany the minister to France for a conference on housing and concrete. The minister's prior experience before his rise in the communist party was said to have been shoe repair and he spoke only Hungarian and Russian. Besides the architectural expertise that was his, my father was also needed because he alone on the trip could speak French and navigate the minister through official receptions. He was also needed because he was considered to have the right "taste" to purchase dress fabric and perfume for the minister's fat Russian wife back home. It was on that trip that he "collected" some money owed to him before the war and purchased an old used car – a Citroën, the sort of black car one sees in silver screen movies. Only communist magistrates, doctors, and my father had a car in Budapest at that time. All the neighborhood children got a ride in it. Evidently my father knew how far he could go within the system and tried to recreate our former style of living to the best of his ability.

The most amazing thing that came his way was a vineyard. It was owned by an elderly couple who were given visas to emigrate to Australia to be with their children. They could not sell it and for some reason the government did not take it. My father, as a friend of the old couple, became a permanent manager of it. We did not own it but we could use it. A peasant family lived on the premises and took care of all the farm chores. I remember several summers at the village of Szabadszállás (Freelodging) in the very comfortable – although without indoor plumbing – main house. It had a lovely veranda with the view of a haystack in the yard. My father was there for the harvest, and we had grapes, fruit, wine, and above-mentioned half of a pig in the Budapest bathtub through the bounty of the vineyard farm.

Given this preferential treatment, my parents' main worry was that the communists would insist that my father enter the party and play a political role. This he did want to do both for ideological and practical reasons. In his mind he still belonged to the Smallholders Party. It is well known how viciously the communists killed each other in purges in their own intrigues and my father did not want to move in the party ranks also because it was extremely dangerous. He had been given the most prestigious Kossuth Prize, kept mostly for party members, and there was a question of how long he would be allowed to hold out. This fear of the party was one reason for leaving the country. When giving advice to me about professions in the US, my father distilled his life in these words: "Never rise too high anywhere, for there is jealousy and intrigue at the top," and "Select a practical profession – doctor or engineer – that has a skill that is valued in any regime; that way you are always needed."

In the US my father read and underlined Márai's expatriate books in which he berates in the most vitriolic language how anyone who stayed in Hungary and worked for the communists was an accessory to crime and helped to prop up a brutal regime. From the underlinings it is likely that my father agreed with this point of view, though at the same time he must have thought that it was easy for Márai to be so judgmental since he wasn't there. What would he have done had he been there? But my father did not have a ruminative temperament and had an ability to live in the present. When he made it to New York, he was in New York, which opened up another era with its own problems, difficulties and satisfactions, and he entered into all that with enthusiasm and optimism.

My father was fifty-six when he came to New York and he imagined that for the third time in his life he would have a successful career. But America was very different from Budapest in ways he hadn't imagined. I think he imagined America to be like a very big European country where he would be at home. He had to learn English, which he did relatively fast and well enough. He had to unlearn the metric system and adapt to the English system of measurements, which he also did. He thought that his distinguished status as a well-known Hungarian architect would give him a privileged position here. He believed in the American ideal of the merit system. He threw himself into work. With another Hungarian architect friend (Lászlo Acsay), they entered a competition to redesign Lafayette Square fronting the White House in Washington. I have the photo mock ups of the square with the suggestion of arched entrances to the roads and a variety of high, low, and intermediate structures in the background. Naturally, they did not win. They were not part of the American architectural establishment – they came out of the blue. In fact, the Lafayette Square project was never built. This project is an indication of the enthusiasm my father brought to America. He immediately embarked on the courses and work necessary to get his architect's license in New York State and was, he said proudly, the only refugee architect to get his license.

The real problem, which he did not realize, was that in America, unlike Europe, most building is not designed by architects but by build-ers. Ordinary buildings, houses, apartment blocks, hotels do not require architects. The architecture schools graduate scores of young talented architects who have mostly nowhere to go. There are great American architects like Frank Lloyd Wright, but their work is a luxury and not a necessity. The competition for any kind of position in architecture is fierce. My father would have had a hard time finding a job of any kind if it had not been for the help of the Szent-Györgyis. They knew someone who recommended him to Wallace K. Harrison, head of the Harrison and Abramowitz firm, one of the largest in New York. He got that job as draughtsman because he was a distinguished refugee architect they were interested in helping and because he also happened to be very good. From then on he was a hired hand. Wallace Harrison received major commissions – he had built the UN building, the Columbia Law School and was about to begin Lincoln Center. These commissions came to him partly because he was related to the Rockefellers. He married Ellen Milton, a Rockefeller on her mother's side, and did a lot of institutional building. Harrison was not the sort that books are written about and classes are taught on in architectural school. He was generally considered to be competent if uninspired. But he had a large office and employed a lot of architects and my father worked there for the rest of his life.

The architectural license was not good for much – he designed one summer house in Sparta, New Jersey, for a wealthy Hungarian who admired him. Otherwise, he was busy with minor additions or refurbishings for small Hungarian businesses in New York. They paid little, if at all. One I remember was the Paprika restaurant whose kitchen had to be redesigned due to health violations. The owner did not pay but we could eat there for free as much as we wanted to. Another was the Hungarian House, meant to be sort of a club for Hungarians, where he ended up doing the work with much dissension for nothing. My mother grumbled.

My father did not show his disappointment. He forbade discussion of the revolution and we never talked about how and why we came to the US. He seemed happy with the daily round of work, meals, family. He got joke books in English. He said more and more that it was up to his daughters, that it was all for his daughters. From a position in the center of things he was now on the sidelines and he enjoyed observing. He didn't necessarily like everything about America, but it was a great adventure to have been here and to have been a part of it and he valued it. He and other elderly Hungarian refugees got together in the Hungarian House and gave lectures and parties. I have a handwritten manuscript of his talk on "American Building Practices" in Hungarian. Or they'd talk about who should run Hungary after communism is over and they often came back to Otto von Hapsburg, a scion of the Austrian royal house who was now a politician. Otto often came and gave a talk at the Hungarian House and everyone was nostalgic for the turn of the century and the greatness of the Austro-Hungarian empire.

Towards the end of his life my father was concerned about religion. He had been secular all his life and often said that since the Enlightenment in the eighteenth century it was not possible for a rational mind to believe in religion. We were a secular family wondering if there might be a god. My father read various books on the subject that I inherited and I can see what ideas he was mulling over. Bertrand Russell's *Why I am not a Christian* had a powerful effect on him as did a then popular book, *The Passover Plot*, which sought to demystify the gospels. It seems that the more he searched for a God or religious certainty, the more it eluded him. These books indicated that behind the enlightenment modernity he had great concerns about what was to happen after death and I don't know if he found anything sustaining.

The end came sooner than he expected. At age seventy-one he noticed strange symptoms such as tremors and an inability to concentrate on the numbers necessary to work out the details of a building on the Albany Mall that Harrison designed with "not a straight line." He was very proud of being the only one in the office who could do it. Suddenly he was unable to do it. He was diagnosed with a type of Parkinson's disease and refused to believe it. He immediately decided to go to Hungary to have brother Dezső examine him. By 1970 Hungary had changed. The communists were still in power, but small trade was allowed, and artists could speak up to a point. It was known as "goulash communism" with the irony that that's what the revolution accomplished. Most important of all, Kadar, the leader of the country, "forgave" all those who left the country in 1956 and allowed them to return for visits. This was not exactly selfless, in that the visitors would bring much needed foreign currency into the country. There was no fear of another revolution. My father applied for a visa, convinced that he would not be allowed back because of his important role in the country. He was actually crestfallen when the visa came with no problems and it was evident that back in

Hungary he no longer mattered. The news from Dezso was worse: he did have Parkinson's disease.

My father died at age seventy-four, bitterly disappointed and sad. He somehow thought that like his father, he would live into his eighties; Feri and Dezső were still alive. He had imagined his old age surrounded by his children and grandchildren in a happy retirement. During the three years he was retired, he was ill, unable to control his body, light bulbs breaking in his hands. He died in the hospital unable to speak, a pitiful look in his eyes. He had just enough money in the bank to cover burial expenses. A great many people came to his funeral to honor him.

2
Countess of Transylvania

"A woman should not be respected for what she does but for what she is."

At the Budapest Academy of Dramatic Arts her classmates dubbed my mother "the countess" because they though that she looked down her nose at them. And maybe she did. According to her own story by the age of ten little Klara criticized her mother for dressing badly with too many flounces and flowers in the way of the provinces. Klara Konya had an incredible sense of style which did not endear her to her mother who in any case preferred her older brothers. Her father, Imre, doted on her and took her to see all the new movies as they came out of Hollywood. As a child, a production entitled *The Geisha* impressed her so much that she walked around with a tablecloth on her slender body for days imitating it. She was going to go on the stage come hell or high water.

My mother came from Marosvásárhely (The Marketplace by the River Maros, Targu Mures in present day Romania), a small provincial town in Transylvania. Transylvania was the largest Hungarian-speaking area that was lost in the treaty of Versailles-Trianon and again after the Second World War. Beautifully wooded and mountainous, with quaint regional customs, Hungarians have always thought of Transylvania as an enchanted place. In the early twentieth century it was famous for its summer artistic colonies and most recently famous for its Asiatic-sounding folk songs that seem to have preserved an archaic Hungary. (They can be heard in the background of a recent movie, *The English Patient.*) When we came to America, however, most Americans associated Transylvania with Dracula and mentioned this to my mother whenever she said where she was from. My mother was horrified – we knew little about Dracula and thought the 1931 film an amusing joke. No one read much English literature – mostly Continental authors were favored – and Bram Stoker's Dracula was quite unknown. The English writer Bram Stoker created Dracula and vampires on the basis of a Romanian ruler known as "Vlad the Impaler," a cruel sixteenth century figure at war with the Turks. His castle is now a major tourist site in Romanian Transylvania. Vlad however had nothing to do with Transylvania, he was from Wallachia. It was the genius of Bram Stoker to have placed this nightmarish figure into a nearby romantic place called Transylvania not knowing how much he'd upset Hungarians ever after. (I don't believe Bram Stoker ever went there.) The upsetting thing to my mother was that Americans seemed to take the Transylvanian location of Dracula literally as the truth. Since Americans could not be talked out of the Dracula myth in "Transylvania," my mother would eventually grimace and say, "I am Dracula!" But even without Dracula, coming from remote and aristocratic Transylvania was exotic in the Budapest Academy of Dramatic Arts and I imagine my mother made the most of it without actually having to suggest that she was, or was not, a countess.

Because it was not possible to travel to Transylvania in Romania during communism – we went once – I never got to know that side of my family except through my mother's stories which seemed like legends not quite verifiable by facts and experience. Konya is the name of an important Turkish town, and my grandfather's name, Konya, coupled with his very dark hair and eyes, made my sister wonder if he had some Turkish ancestry, which of course in Hungary with several hundred years of Turkish occupation is quite possible. Transylvania had a special deal with the Turks – they accepted their overlordship in exchange for local autonomy, and that period was a major flowering of Hungarian arts and letters only in Transylvania. Transylvania had kept Hungary alive. Transylvania was a remarkably tolerant place where German and Hungarian Calvinists, Catholics, Romanian Orthodox Christians as well as Turks lived in reasonable harmony. However, my grandfather Konya came from Debrecen in eastern Hungary from a family with many children. In Transylvania he taught Latin and Greek. He was a sweet guy.

My mother's stories of his mother's family were so convoluted that I always got lost in them. First there was the confusion in the name. The "nemes" in Anna Nemes literally meant "noble," but was a common Hungarian name. Depending on how my mother told her tales we were descended either from nobility or from a family called "noble." Accounts of family history seemed to go back to a well-to-do estate manager on some huge estate of a very important count – a big house, many servants, wonderful delicacies like peeled plum jam. Her grand-parents seemed to have lived in a kind of ante-bellum luxury and order in a place that was paradise. You can't quarrel with that vision. Her grandparents and aunts and uncles were numerous and hard to keep track of. She liked mentioning a successful uncle who owned a sugar refinery and had mistresses. In the one photo I have of the clan he sits conspicuously at the far left in a light (white?) suit. My mother is in the foreground with the other children, immediately recognizable by her sulking expression. The clan is seated outside and a rich floral rug had been brought out for them that is incongruous with the trees in the back. Evidently the photo required outside light and a long exposure. My mother must have been eight or nine. The photo must date from 1927 or 1928 but looks more like something out of the end of the nineteenth century. And the way my mother talked, the beauties of that era were identical to the time before the First World War. I always felt that the late nineteenth century and the Twenties and Thirties were, in the minds of my parents, one great time of opulence, tradition, and fulfillment that the two wars interrupted so cruelly. Reality was not always so idyllic.

Actually, my mother was not born in Transylvania, because my grandmother went into labor at a time of panicky escape in a railroad cattle car in Hungary and she was born in the cattle car. After the Versailles-Trianon Treaty, Romania re-annexed Transylvania and menaced the Hungarian population, many of whom fled from their brutality. Coexistence eventually returned and the family went back for a period of peaceful living in Romania. My mother continued to dream of the stage against her parents' wishes who thought of it as a disreputable profession. Her mother was a small town lady busy with her women's circle and charitable activities. My mother dreamed of leaving the provincial town of Marosvásárhely for Budapest. To her being an actress was something modern and it went with the stylishly modern clothes she preferred, and to her the very center of modernity was in Budapest and points west. She won the battle and entered the Academy of Dramatic Arts in Budapest, living with a well-known retired actress who was a family friend (Aranka Hettyei). In a short career she played minor roles of ingénues and was apparently good in drawing room comedies. With her spectacular looks – blonde hair, blue eyes, slender and graceful figure – she did some modeling and might have gone to serious success had she not married my father and given up the stage. She always said she gave up the stage because of the casting couch – not being willing to go to bed with directors and producers. But it was also clear that the world of the theatre had ruthlessly ambitious people and complex human relations in which drive and an ability to negotiate were also essential. Those she did not have. At one point a director took her aside and told her gently that "talent was not enough."

The really big drama in my mother's life was meeting and marrying my father and that too was as long and confusing a story as the account of her ancestors. Like her birth, it too had to do with the changing political relationship of Transylvania and Romania. Because of Hitler's pact with Hungary, for a short while Transylvania was re-annexed to Hungary. My mother had a plum theatrical role: she was to play in "Queen Irene," a play mounted during the celebration festivities in the most important Transylvanian city of Kolozsvár (Cluj). This was a story that took place in the Byzantine Empire about a ruthless queen who blinded and murdered her son and took the throne herself. I doubt that my mother had the lead but probably she had lovely Byzantine style gilded costumes to set off her looks in a lesser role. She was on an unscheduled special train from Budapest that carried various dignitaries to the event and required special permission for her to ride. She was making good back home in Transylvania near her parents and must have felt triumphant. As yet unknown to her, my father was also on the train to meet his brother, Dezső, who was a neurologist in Kolozsvár. I no longer remember why he was on the special train, but he had special permission, too. Anyhow, according to her story when they got off, there was such a crowd that all the horse-drawn cabs were gone except for one which they both claimed. My father suggested that they should share it, but my mother would not share it with a "stranger" even after she insisted that he "identify" himself and gave him a hard time. In the end, of course, she did share the cab, and it eventually turned out that my mother knew his brother because she had been "sort of "going out" with Dezső. The comparison between Dezső and Laci was, from a woman's point of view, to my father's advantage in every way.

When I knew my uncle Dezső later in life he was a serious, heavy-set man. Unlike my father who was joking his way through life, Dezső was a serious researcher obsessed with his work and deeply involved in the Catholic religion he grew up in. To my childish eyes he seemed very worthy but very dull. I was never surprised that his wife, Marta, had left him for the glamorous Albert Szent-Györgyi who received the Nobel Prize in 1937 in biochemistry for, among other things, the synthesis of Vitamin C. Marta also came from Baja, married the then dashing young Dezső and they had two children, Orsi and Gabor. Dezső and Albert were both working in the research institutes of Szeged, a town east of Baja in southern Hungary. Szent-Györgyi synthesized Vitamin C out of peppers, partly because Szeged was a big paprika-producing area and there were a lot of peppers about. Albert was a clever and lively person who enjoyed all the good things in life. During the war, as a very visible Nobel Laureate he spoke out against Nazism, making him the target of the Gestapo. He hid in the Swedish embassy and was freed by the Russians. He thereupon went to Moscow where he wanted to see Stalin personally. In everything that he did, Albert was larger than life. The affair between him and Marta developed in Szeged and had become a major scandal. Dezső did not want to divorce, Marta did, and there was a problem of what to do with their children. It was at this time that Dezső went to Transylvania and got to know my mother. The situation was messily unresolved. Despite having been a womanizing bachelor, my father had Victorian morals and refused to speak to Marta or even of Marta. After my parents were married they had to take care of little Gabor and Orsi because Albert and Marta emigrated to the US in 1947 without them. Eventually the children followed them to Woods Hole in Cape Cod. For my father, who idolized his older brother, this was a terrible event. Dezső stayed in Transylvania and married a real countess Toldalaghy (she was not only a countess by marriage but also by birth) who gave birth to one child and was subsequently paralyzed for the rest of her life. That son, Ambrus, who grew up mostly in Romania is now a professor of Romanian history at the major university in Budapest. There are no surviving Miskolczy sons – Gabor and Ambrus both had daughters.

There is no question that my father, a dynamic and cheerful bachelor, was more suited to my mother than the melancholy scientist in the midst of a divorce with two children. At the age of forty-two my father may have been ready to settle down with the beautiful twenty-three year old actress. They had in common their interest in modernity and in the visual arts of architecture, theater, furnishing, clothes. I suspect that she was very good at attracting him by pretending to repulse him, and the brief rivalry with his brother helped. My father was much too jaded by women throwing themselves at him to be attracted by coming on directly. Evidently he wanted his "countess." They married in Maros-vásárhely in the middle of the war in 1942. When the topic of their courtship and marriage came up, he would always say: "I had to marry her, what was she going to do with those skinny legs!"

Life on the stage ended abruptly as I was born in 1943, the siege of Budapest came in 1944, and my sister, Kristina, was born in 1945. After my birth my mother seemed to have had violent post-partum depression; she talked of screaming while nursing me and a baby nurse took care of me. We were then living on the top floor of an apartment building in Marko Street by the Danube and I assume the cellar to come was there or nearby. My mother said that when I was born they had a staff of five servants and the task of one woman was exclusively to cook for me especially since I suffered from constant digestive difficulties. It must have been a large apartment. I don't know why we did not go back there after the siege, but we then moved to Buda to Otto Herman Street to the top floor of an unfinished villa my father finished in lieu of rent. Strangely enough my mother got well and strong during the siege, cooking for dozens, but was off and on unwell throughout my childhood. All the doctor friends of Dezső who were consulted could recommend were sleeping cures and rest. During communism almost all women had to work but my mother did not and perhaps could not. My father was proud that he could support the family by himself. In retrospect I think my mother was somewhat mentally ill, perhaps bipolar, but in those days it was not recognized and not treated. Most treatments for such illnesses even in the US date only from the 1970's. My mother was sometimes depressed and talked of suicide. She was sometimes agitated and screamed about this or that. Sometimes she was quite well and took us to the swimming pools in Budapest, went to the dressmakers, got together with friends, some of whom did not work for various reasons. She taught the maids how to cook her kind of more sophisticated food. We had dinner parties, my parents went to the theater, they took us to the puppet theater. Throughout communism she was a semi-invalid who lived a comfortable and sheltered life in which she found many joys.

She was excellent in needlework, knitting, and especially embroidery. She made Kristina and me dresses with blouses embroidered in the style of Kalocsa peasants – colorful flowers on a white ground. She herself had a Kalocsa-style outfit made in Kalocsa before the war that had the most exquisite white lace apron to go with it. (Kalocsa is about an hour's drive north of Baja.) It was fashionable in the nineteen thirties and forties to admire primitive and peasant art because it seemed so much like modern art. Kodaly and Bartok collected peasant music. My father had photographed peasant architecture and published a book about it. My father and Uncle Feri even started a rug workshop at Kalocsa and designed modern rugs on the basis of peasant art in an attempt to revive traditional crafts. One of these beautiful rugs is in my living room here in New York. Peasant art was seen as the originator of the modern and beautiful in its simplicity. At the same time, peasant art stood for tradition and for a specific Hungarian spirit and unfortunately was vanishing under the onslaught of modernization. The communists hated peasant culture as part of the old class system and nationalism, and did their best to extirpate it in collective farms and by a disapproval of native dress. My mother embroidering us Kalocsa-style dresses was both a form of nationalism, nostalgia, and resistance. She encouraged all forms of resistance that did not cost you your life. Unfortunately one of her brothers in Romania fought the communists head on and disappeared, probably murdered in the 1950's. His body was never recovered. Like everyone else, my mother walked a narrow line between survival and resistance. The communists didn't kill peasant art completely – I remember seeing people in regional dress in my childhood. What killed it was television and recent capitalism. People now work in the fields in cheap but cosmopolitan track suits.

The happiest time in my mother's life was in Otto Herman Street under communism. She was taken care of, she had a family, she had friends, she had outlets for her creativity. She was concerned about communism but in the end it did not harm her directly. Her disabilities were manageable in this context. Finally, she was still young and very beautiful. In the US my mother fell apart.

For a while in the US my mother tried to find something to do that made money since that was essential. Even more than under communism, here all refugee Hungarian women had to work. Because she did not work and did not come into contact with enough Americans, she had trouble learning English. My father had a job and she had to keep house for him. Often he came home for lunch. She tried various artistic projects. At one point she tried painting on silk for scarves, but this was before such luxury items were popular. With an American friend of my sister's, she was going to go into a lingerie/hostess dress design business in the summer vacation spot of Lenox, Massachusetts, and a great many beautiful things were made for that, none of which sold. American women were not yet wearing silk slips. All this would have done well in the Eighties when Americans had money and liked sophisticated things, but not in the late Fifties and early Sixties. There was talk of merchandising our barbecue sauce made of paprika and wine which had the same fate of being unpractical. My father made enough money so she didn't have to be a cleaning lady or a cashier for which, in any case, she didn't have the physical strength. After my father died and she was alone with no money, she went to all the florist shops on the East Side asking if they would not have a job for her arranging flowers.

Kristina and I were away at boarding school, she had lost her old friends and it was not easy making new friends when everyone worked all day and was exhausted at night. She was alone at first in a dingy small apartment I remember being all green, and even when in a better place, it was nowhere near the grand Otto Herman Street home with its huge terrace and view of the mountain. There was no point in getting elegantly dressed for the supermarket or the drugstore. She enjoyed discount department stores where she searched for stylish clothes for us hidden like needles in a haystack of tasteless junk. She would mail those along with homemade cookies to the boarding schools we were in. Then she would sit down in front of the TV to watch "I Love Lucy" whose artistry she appreciated as a former actress. Lucy did not require much English. Then she waited for my father to come home from work.

She became an alcoholic slowly and gradually. My father believed that wine had curative powers. He was a connoisseur of Hungarian and French wine, most of which he could not afford in the US. But he knew how to choose the good wines among the cheap ones and had a glass or two with dinner and if he came home for lunch. If anything ailed my mother – and a great deal did – he would say: "Klara, have another glass of wine." My sister and I blamed my father for my mother's alcoholism which he did not seem to recognize. After he died my mother got worse. She was sometimes delirious and called up in the middle of the night that a Turk and a little girl were in her room. My sister decided that she could not stay in New York and took her to live in Bethlehem, Pennsylvania, where she was living. We tried AA-type rehabilitation, but she was not willing. After one of those typical meetings where recovering alcoholics talk about their addiction in graphic terms, she got up and said that she didn't want to have anything to do with such disgusting people and why was she there anyway? Bethlehem had the advantage that she could not get alcohol. A small stroke left her with difficulty walking and she was surrounded by people who would not get it for her. For the last two decades of her life she lived there. Miracle of miracles, she sobered up and was mostly sober for that time. She never admitted to being an alcoholic and there were slippages when a new neighbor might get her the gallon of Gallo for her "family get-together." The other great benefit of Bethlehem was that her English improved greatly because there were no Hungarians around. For the first time she could be somewhat a part of American life. It is to Kristina's credit that my mother lived until the age of seventy-six and had some joy in her later years even though, as it turned out, mother and younger daughter did not get on too well.

I got to know my mother well during her sober years in Bethlehem. I visited there and she often stayed with me in New York or in our country house in Pennsylvania for up to a month. At that time I was divorced and sometimes my mother was my only companion. She was a fantastic companion; I can see why my father doted on her. She was there when you wanted afternoon tea or any other kind of companionship and she went to have a nap, knit, or read so you could have solitude. She baked wonderful goodies from the old country with evocative names like "non plus ultra" or my favorite, "lady's whim." Lady's whim was a square layer of melt-in-your-mouth buttery pastry with apricot jam on top and above that a meringue. It tasted sort of like a version of lemon meringue pie because of the tartness of the apricot jam. Some chocolate-nutty confections had the name of Hungarian restaurants before the war. While we had tea she regaled me with stories of the war, before the war, and of her family at the turn of the century. We discussed my romances which she thought I handled very badly. She was very proud of me for being a professor at Columbia University but she would have been happier if I had been a movie star or the wife of a prominent man. She always advised that I should marry a self-made man because they are the best. She was against the current version of feminism that sent every woman into the workplace as a way of shoring up her self-esteem. She said many times that a woman should be respected not for what she does but for what she is. One could say that she said this because it had not been possible for her to work outside the home but all I had to do was to look around me and see the desperate desire for success that young women had and to compare that with my mother's dignity and sense of self-worth. Here was this alcoholic woman of no great accomplishment who was a remarkable human being. This is not to say that at times, even sober, she could be hysterical, mean, demanding and totally impossible.

My mother's most awesome trait was her insight into people. She could read your thoughts and emotions before you had them. She was brilliant and uncanny, and my father, whose radar was simpler, relied on my mother's insight to navigate through the shoals of communism in Hungary and the new world in New York. She knew things as she knew how her mother ought to dress at the age of ten. My mother basically wore less than a dozen items of clothing all of which were the most right for her in terms of elegance and managed to be appropriate to a lady in her seventies who sometimes looked sixteen. I have closets full of mistakes I don't wear. (I sent her a lot of my hand-me-downs, and while she enjoyed looking at them, mostly they hung in her closet.) I don't know who I am and what I should look like the way my mother did. She was like that in many areas of her life. Her insight was quick as lightning. When this insight came in a negative mood she was cruel and I thought of her as a witch. In another era she might have been burned at the stake.

Another reason my sister wanted to take my mother away from New York was that after my father's death, Klara seemed to have developed romantic feelings towards their family doctor and worse, it seemed like he returned them. Kristina thought my mother drank excessively in order to be sick to see the doctor and doctor did not help her kick the habit because he liked her too much. (Of course the doctor was a married man with grown children.) It is possible that the doctor did not help, although I don't think anyone could have stopped my mother's alcoholism. The only thing one could do, which my sister did, was to quarantine her. Not surprisingly, my mother went to Bethlehem kicking and screaming. She hated ending up in a "provincial" city like the "provincial" city where she came from as if she had achieved nothing. She loved living in New York – the center of the world – even if she did not take advantage of museums or theatres. She hated being separated from the doctor, a genial, tall, grey haired man her own age who romanced her in Hungarian. One of the big attractions of coming to visit me in New York was the doctor who came over for an hour or two, fumbled with his stethoscope for a while and settled down to chat. I served drinks and let them be. It had never been a physical relationship because they were old and my mother was squeamish; it was a romance. They were going over old times, my mother's current physical symptoms, and he often recited to her his own poetry in Hungarian. At Christmas she bought him gifts, like gloves. This "love affair" went on at long intervals for many years and made my mother happy. The doctor was her soul mate whether he was there or not. On her last visit to New York when she suspected that she might die in the near future, even though that was quite some time away, she and the doctor said a formal goodbye forever. She waved him goodbye without a tearful scene.

Her ability to find joy and companionship in the most difficult circumstances was evident in the nursing home where she spent the last few years of her life. It was an adequate place we could afford in Bethlehem, but nothing grand since she had no money and we were supporting her. She kicked and screamed about going there, too, but she needed the supervision. The staff consisted of young women who despite her obviously difficult behavior liked my mother. They put up with her airs, brought her trays in bed so she would not have to go down to the dining room. My mother was generally an exotic creature in staid Bethlehem and once more played the role of countess which everyone seemed to enjoy. The young women made friends with her and confided to her their problems with their boyfriends, their husbands, their mothers, their outfits. Especially when we were not in hearing distance and she did not have to prove how much she hated the nursing home, she was happily giving out advice and seeing the young women through their difficulties.

My mother died from liver failure brought on by drinking. Kristina called me to say that she didn't have much time left and I should visit her. When I came, my mother seemed no worse than usual but she said matter-of-factly that she was dying. There was nothing for her to leave, what little costume jewelry she had she had given to us a long time ago. There were no practicalities to discuss. So we just chatted for an hour or so as we always did though we were both moved. Eventually a hospice attendant came in with a portable toilet and asked her to use it and she got up to do so. She started to fumble with her clothes and then she changed her mind, turned to me and asked me to leave. We hugged warmly because that was goodbye even with the attendant there. I left because I knew that she told me to go because she wanted to spare me seeing the messiness of her condition which included her dying. She told me to go because she wanted me to remember her still well and on her feet. And it's true – I remember her standing in a pink nightdress and robe and looking at me with probing and intelligent eyes out of a face that could have been sixteen. In a few days she went into a coma and in another few she died.

My mother had courage.

3
Childhood Under Communism

Talpra Magyar, hi a haza!   *On your feet, Hungarian, your country calls!*
Itt az ido, most vagy soha!   *Here is the time, now or never!*

Sándor Petőfi, 1848

I have sometimes been asked whether I had a happy childhood or not and I have never known what to answer. The first memory I have at about age five is of being shaken by my French governess, Anni, yelling in my ears, "Pênche-toi, pênche-toi" (Bend over, bend over). I was sitting at the dining room table being rather aggressively shaken and exhorted to bend over the soup or something and not to make a mess. We had a French governess living with us since I was at least two so that we could grow up bilingual. Hungarian is a wonderful and much beloved language but only about fifteen million speak it and it is too hard for the rest to learn. Most Hungarian middle and upper class parents taught their children a foreign language which was usually German because the immediate neighbors in Austria and Germany spoke German. Austria had also been the partner in the former Austro-Hungarian empire. It was assumed that in the course of time we would also learn German because it was natural. My parents were unusual in selecting French rather than German to begin with, which indicated their wider horizons and aspirations – they wanted us to speak two foreign languages. Starting us so young was also unusual: Kristina spoke French before she spoke Hungarian. My parents were obviously aware of the fact that languages are best learned when very, very young, probably the then current educational theory. My French is instinctive and very good even when dormant most of the time and I appreciate having it. It adds another dimension to my life. However I did not appreciate Anni, who was something of a sadist disciplinarian and who had enormous power over us in the early years.

All the adults in my childhood seemed to be disciplinarians. According to funny stories told by my parents I used to use my potty as a vehicle to ride not knowing what else to do with it. There seems to have been an emphasis on precociously young learning and serious sanctions when one did not obey. My father grew up with the rod and he did not spare us. His approach was particularly galling because he did not seem angry. Quite calmly he would say: "My dear daughter, would you go get the rod." And I would have to get the bamboo rod kept for that purpose in the corner of the room. He would then beat us until it hurt quite a lot. If we cried he said: "If you cry I will beat you more." We learned to bear pain without crying. Then when it was over and the rod was put back, he would say: "Come over and give your father a kiss. I am not angry with you." That was the worst part because whether he was angry or not, I was. And what were beaten for? Mostly for little things. Lying would merit a beating because honesty was considered the highest value. But in general I was an honest child. Of course in the life of children and adults lying is often necessary and one thing I ultimately learned from the beatings was how to lie well because the stakes were high. Another reason we were beaten was if we had upset my mother. My mother was fragile, she needed rest every afternoon after lunch, and we had to play very quietly so as not to wake or irritate her. This was not always possible.

While my mother generally took our side against my father's beatings, she herself had a temper and could fly into a rage, giving out sudden and unexpected slaps on the face (known as "pofon") that could smart and turn your cheek red. I don't remember all the reasons but I know that once it was because of a messy closet. The fact was, we were very good young girls not creating any serious mischief, and were dealt with rather harshly.

The only person in the household who was not a disciplinarian was usually the maid. We had a maid's room by the kitchen and generally had a succession of country girls as maids. They provided us with access to cookies and easygoing conversation. We made such friends with the maids that one invited us to spend two weeks in her village one summer. That was one of the highlights of my childhood. The name of the village was Markota-Bödöge, and I don't know precisely where it was. The houses were all thatched and we played with the neighboring children in the barns or in some swimming hole. It was harvest time and we got to ride on top of hay carts. One highlight of the trip was a fire in the village which was put out by old-fashioned horse-drawn fire engines. By the time we went home we looked like the other dirty peasant urchins and announced happily to my mother: "Mommy, Mommy, we didn't have to bathe or brush our teeth the whole time!"

When I was older I was fascinated by the clothes the maids wore on their day off or with their boyfriends. My mother was always very elegant in form-fitting custom-made suits in understated dove greys and sky blues. I often admired her great beauty. The maids liked flashy stuffs in shiny silks and bright colors – reds and yellows – with full skirts with lots of swishing material on their full hips. One dress I still see in my mind's eye is white with great big red tulips all over it. I knew that these were in very bad taste, that I should never wear such a thing, but I admired their very loudness. It is worth noting that in the 1950's synthetics were not yet available in Hungary so the maid actually wore silk. Nylon things first came in in the care packages of used clothes sent by Marta from the US. I remember one white see-through blouse made the rounds among all my mother's friends with everyone admiring this great, new, exotic material. Sometimes the exotic is just the rare and not inherently valuable. Just like savages who fell in love with glass beads, women in Budapest oohed and aahed over nylon. And yet my mother had all her and our clothes custom made by seamstresses out of wonderful natural materials like wool, cotton, and silk. Most of the stuff in Marta's packages we gave away because they were too worn or shapeless and we did not want them.

My father managed to create a domestic life that was not terribly different from an upper middle class life in the 1930's. We had a spectacular apartment on the top floor of a villa overlooking a mountain, with a spacious terrace, sometimes used for cleaning and cutting peas, strawberries or peaches for canning by my mother, the maid, and us children working together. Canned foods were either not available or not very good quality and we canned most of our own, just as my father made our own sausages at times. Someone came from the country selling fresh milk products such as sour cream and cottage cheese. We made our own yoghurt. When we left in November 1956 we left a larder full of the most delicious jams, fruits, vegetables, and other foodstuffs. This is not to say that there weren't food shortages under the communists and one constantly had to be on the lookout for what was available to stock up on

it. Meat was periodically scarce and we had many imaginatively prepared vegetarian meals. In general, my parents' attitude seems to have
been that they were not going to be stopped by life under communism.
Surely it would end and "real" life would continue.

In the apartment there was one very large room with a living area at
the end near the windows and a dining table at the other end near the
kitchen. Besides the large Persian rugs and the bookshelf there was a
small crystal bar cart that gave out a jingling sound. It was often a
problem when I tried to sneak a book out of my parents' bookshelf
without being heard. My parents and my sister and I each had a large
room. The apartment was originally larger, but if someone had a large
apartment the communists moved in another family. Sharing a bathroom
and kitchen with another family was a nightmare and my father cut off
the equivalent of another apartment out of ours and gave it up
voluntarily. I don't remember those rooms at all. With this it seems we
were not bothered with the possibility of lodgers being moved in, at least
as far as I am aware.

When I look back on my childhood, it seems nineteenth century
with the servants (I must not forget the woman who came to wash and
iron once a week in the absence of washing machines), the home prepa-
ration of old-fashioned foods, the natural fibers and the craftsmen and
craftswomen who made our clothes and furniture. If I went outside, that
was old-fashioned, too, in the absence of cars. In our area there were
only two, my father's and that of a man across the street. Everything was
on horse-drawn vehicles; coal for heating and other heavy weights were
carried by bulky horses with drivers yelling and cracking their whips on
the poor sweating animals. Much commerce in the city was on the backs
of horses, although tramways and streetcars moved people since the
nineteen hundreds and buses were now the norm. But most of the now
existing Budapest subway system was built decades after we left. (A
small section had been built about 1900, one of the first subways in the
world.) When I look at the BBC movies of Sherlock Holmes I am
reminded of the Hungary of my childhood.

I remember the first day of school and going through the big
wrought iron gates of its garden. School was wonderful in that reading
and writing unlocked the universe for me. Although school was authori-
tarian, other kids behaved so much worse that I that I had no problems

with the teachers. Our class of about thirty-five was seated in three rows of double benches nailed to the floor by height from front to rear. Since I was tall I was always in the very back sharing a bench with Edda Ertl who was even taller than I was and who thus became my best friend. The teacher's desk and chair were on a platform so she could look over us and see who misbehaved. At all normal times or for discipline we had to sit with our arms behind our backs. This was supposed to improve our posture and keep our hands out of trouble. But, the communists did not believe in corporal punishment so there were no switches or rulers or hands being applied to the students. If you misbehaved you got a little booklet with a warning not to take home to your parents known as an (intő) and if your parents beat you up, that was their business. At one point the school put us all in uniforms – dark blue pinafores over white blouses and the regulation red communist kerchief. Characteristically, my mother was not satisfied with this and had her dressmaker reinterpret it in better cotton with little ruffles on the edges. I was mortified to have to wear such a fancy outfit and would have preferred to look like everyone else. However, as I was always told, I was "different" and had to live with that. The difference of the pinafores raised eyes but caused no problems in the school.

Learning was based on recitation and you could be called upon at any time at the whim of the teacher. Whatever class it was, there had to be some reference to the greatness of the Soviet Union. Suppose you were reciting a lesson in botany class about the classification of fruits, you first had to start out by saying that this classification was invented by the great Russian scientist X and that the Soviet Union was making great strides in the improvement of – well, you could say anything – fruits, classifications, whatever. Similarly in math class the theorem under discussion was attributed to a Soviet mathematician, and once that was out of the way you could do the math. All culture of all times was attributed to the Soviets and it was formulaic – all you had to do was to change the names from one field to another and say the same things. Actually, if you could not remember the names you could just refer to the great Soviet thinkers in general. The teachers, who were probably not communists, did not seem to care what you said, so long as you stuck to the official formula they had to administer. Russian was compulsory and taught by teachers who hardly knew it. After eight years I learned almost nothing and by a mental block later I even forgot that little nothing. We knew that all this veneration of the Soviet Union was a baseless lie and learned it temporarily without really learning it. The great skill I learned in elementary school in communist Hungary was to read between the lines and to focus on the difference between what is said and what is done. Those were the perfect prerequisites for becoming a future art historian. I learned to read images. Parents helped you to know what could be said and what could not be said, but I would say by the first grade we all pretty much knew and did not have to be instructed.

Despite all the emphasis on Soviets and Russians we did have classes in Hungarian history and literature, so long as the formulas were respected. And these classes went deep and were remembered. The history told of the origin of the Hungarian nomads somewhere in Siberia, their migration to Europe in the ninth century, their ruthless successes in raids, their fantastic horsemanship, how they became Western Christians and not Orthodox Easterners and how they settled down in the Carpathian basin. Next came the story of what a great medieval and renaissance kingdom they created under King Matthias and how the Turks came and destroyed it, occupying the country for centuries. They were chased out with the help of Austria, and then the Austrians in their turn came to be overlords in Hungary. The most passionate part of the story was about the 1848 rebellion for independence against Austria which only lasted about a year because the Austrians called in Russian troops to put it down. In the end everyone was ambivalent about the Austro-Hungarian monarchy of the turn of the century since despite the lack of political independence, it was a time of prosperity and a florescence of the arts. Then you had to add ritualistically that it all turned out to be fine because the great Soviet forces liberated Hungary from the German-Austrian yoke in 1945 forever. The word "liberation" had to be extensively used in relation to the Soviets. The end of the war was referred to as "since liberation...."

The only class that did not have an official formula was Hungarian literature class. It was also taught by memorization. For days and weeks we memorized poems, stanza by stanza, until we knew all the famous ones by heart. "Talpra Magyar, hi a haza" ("On your feet Hungarian, your country calls") was one that was written two days before the revolution of 1848 as a call to action. It was written by a favorite poet,

Sándor Petőfi, one of the revolutionary heroes who fought in the 1848 revolution and died mysteriously on the battlefield at a very young age, his body never found. We learned the great epic of Miklos Toldy by János Arany who was a contemporary of Petőfi. The hero of the poem, Toldy, was a great Transylvanian nobleman who fought against the Turks. Hungarians were always fighting against foreign occupiers and writing poems on their defeats. I learned these poems so well that I pick up allusions to them in modern Hungarian TV and cabaret programs even now from a much younger generation still taught the same. "Talpra Magyar" is both taken seriously and is the first line of many jokes.

If you could not rail against the Russians, you could rail against the Turks, and if you made a connection of similarity between them, who could blame you? The Turks were a barbarian, eastern horde occupying a poor little land struggling to keep its religion and culture in the orbit of Western Europe. A little country that by its heroism kept the Turks from getting further West, so that today Austrian and French children do not have to recite poems about their heroes fighting the Turks. Our class went to the National Museum to look at nineteenth century paintings of Hungarian history, and there were many colorful scenes of battles with the Turks. Most memorable was one of the siege of Eger Castle which was also desperately defended by women. When the men ran out of ammunition, the women poured boiling oil on the Turks trying to climb up the side of the hill. I never forgot the image of a heroic woman in a white blouse with bare arms holding a large cauldron. That story was familiar from a beloved children's book, *The Stars of Eger*, which I read more than once. We grew up on the Turkish-Hungarian conflict. If I remember correctly, Eger won that heroic contest, but lost to the next Turkish army soon after. Hungarians are used to losing and putting up heroic defenses nevertheless.

Although the communists were against religion, the word "God" was all right in certain contexts, such as in the Hungarian anthem which we sang in class:

> God bless the Hungarian with plenty and good cheer, give him a protective arm when he struggles with his enemies, he's been tearing his chains for a long time, he has long expiated the sins of the past and future, bring him a new year....

It sounds better in Hungarian because the word for "him" and "her" is the same genderless "ő." It is sung in a dirge-like melody that rises to a wail in the middle. In school, for example, it could be said that "We are lucky to have been liberated by the great Soviet Union in 1945," and then the class could launch into this hymn and ask God to "remove the chains," and if God understood that to be the chains of the Soviets, that was no one's fault. This kind of thing happened all the time and was sometimes full of pathos and sometimes very funny. The mental contradictions the communist edicts put us in in school could be hilarious and we laughed at them openly. With an education system of such transparent duplicity and underlying nationalism it is no wonder that fourteen-year-old boys joined the revolution.

The only girl in my class known to have communist parents was the daughter of the police chief. I remember one incident in which she showed off a ballpoint pen she brought back from the Soviet Union. She bragged that nobody could make a better ballpoint pen than the Soviets. The wiry little daughter of the superintendent of our neighboring villa jumped on the police chief's much bigger daughter, grabbed the pen, took it apart, stomped on it and told her it was a worthless piece of shit to be flushed down the toilet. And she spat on it. Most of the class silently supported the super's daughter. When the police chief caused a fuss the next day, the big and fat wife of the super grabbed the police chief's daughter on the way to school and told her that if she tattled to her father any more she would break every bone in her body. After that the police chief's daughter kept her mouth shut.

We lived in an atmosphere of violence or potential violence. School was less than a ten minute walk from my home but in the dark it was terrifying. For much of the way the road was next to a so-called park, which was actually an abandoned and overgrown piece of land without paved paths or playgrounds. I often overheard adults talk about the terrible crimes that had been committed there, most recently in the form of "undressings" – the aim of the robbers was the clothes of the victims. Unsuspecting passersby were lured into the bushes, stripped, and left there naked. Clothes were obviously hard to come by and there was poverty that became criminal. When I was little I used to run by the park in a panic and even later I never could walk by without my heart racing. Of course the mugger was probably more interested in a man's suit and wallet or woman's handbag than my school pinafore. But the atmosphere of fear was catching and reinforced with all the new stories of crimes that I could overhear from maids, my parents, or the other children. There was also something known as bell-fright (csengő frász) which was much worse. It was the constant fear that when the doorbell rang a member of the secret police, the AVO, would be standing there taking away somebody for torture, death, never to be seen again. No one was immune to bell-fright and we jumped every time the bell rang and we weren't expecting anyone. There did not have to be a reason to be taken away. I heard many who left in 1956 say that they left because of the bell-fright. We, in particular, lived quite well, but over us as over everyone hung a cloud of unpredictability and the secret police. We knew that my mother's brother had been taken away and probably executed in Romania since he never turned up. My father seemed to have found a protected position, but at any moment someone could have turned against him and given his name to the AVO. We were most afraid of doorbells rung in the middle of the night.

Although its effects will be forever unknown to me, I must have spent one of my earliest years in a situation of terror in the cellar during the Second World War. Bombs were falling, I do not know how loud it sounded to a one year old, and the adults must have been upset and preoccupied at the least, if not hysterical. Under communism fear and violence were everyday matters. In my twenties in New York I sometimes woke up with an involuntary and blood-curdling scream coming from my throat for no specific reason that I could explain.

We were brought up on ideas of heroism and sacrifice and little everyday resistances possibly courting disaster. One example was my ponytail hairdo. My mother must have seen that is was fashionable in the West from the women's magazines Marta sent from the US and which were not punishable. So she put my long dark hair that was usually in pigtails in a ponytail. Evidently this was beyond the permitted boundaries because my mother and I were called in to the principal's office and told that the ponytail was a degenerate capitalist, anti-communist hairdo and I must not wear it. She gave us a long lecture. This was just a warning and I was still allowed to wear it occasionally, which I did proudly as a political statement. A good friend of the family, the well-known Hungarian sculptor Béni Ferenczy, did a portrait of me in bronze with the ponytail. This bronze bust is now in the Ferenczy Museum in the artist-town of Szentendre.

I was the elected president of my class but had no duties I can remember. Perhaps I helped line everyone up for the May 1st parades and marched up front. One year we carried flags we had embroidered in class with folk-art designs – an unintentional (?) bit of nationalism. The marches were memorable for the tired, talking, joking, sweating multitudes listening in common to boring talks by communist leaders about outdoing the next Five Year Plans. They were quite bearable on a beautiful day in May, under a blue sky, in the company of the whole class. The incident of the ponytail threatened my presidency. But I finally really lost it when I was confirmed in the Hungarian Reformed Church.

When I was twelve my parents asked me if I wanted to get confirmed or not. This was a strange question in that my parents were not religious at all. My father was christened a Catholic and my mother was a Protestant. The Austrian emperor Franz Josef decreed that in the case of such mixed marriages the children should follow the religion of the parent of the same gender. Since we were girls, we were Protestants. My father joked that that was just as well since he would be a poor religious example for a son. Although we honored the traditions of christenings, marriages and funerals in the church, to my knowledge my parents never went to church on Sunday in Hungary or the US. Christmas was brought to most Catholic Hungarian children by the "Baby Jesus" but to us it came via "the angels." The angels brought the whole flaming tree with real candles and sparklers on it as a surprise. We tried to catch a glimpse of the angel on Christmas Eve but it was always too late. (There was no Santa; St. Nicholas came on December 5th and brought candy or switches depending on whether you were good or bad. He put them in your shoes and you saw them when you woke up.) Perhaps on the basis of the American Santa Claus the communists tried to institute a "Father Winter," but it did not take. Father Winter was mostly a butt of jokes. My non-religious Calvinist-Catholic family had angels. I had a certain nostalgia for organized religion because my friend Edda was a devout Catholic and there was a friendly looking Catholic church not far from us. I sometimes went with her not understanding a word they said in the service but pleased with the beautiful tall angels painted on the walls and the lovely sound of the church bells. I knew also that this was not "my" religion and it was exciting to trespass on someone else's, but basically I had no idea what Christianity was about.

It was obvious that the step of confirmation would not be a religious step but a political one without anyone having to say so. The communists abhorred religion and penalized anyone who was involved in a congregation. The Catholic Cardinal Mindszenty was arrested Christmas 1948 and was living in an AVO prison, tortured and vilified but not killed. Mindszenty was a symbol of Hungarian and religious freedom and resistance. He was released during the 1956 revolution. (He was previously arrested by the Nazis in 1944.)

There was never any real doubt in my mind about being confirmed. Would the woman holding the cauldron of boiling oil over the attacking Turks have hesitated? I went to the necessary Sunday School classes and memorized the required answers to the catechism without any of it having any meaning to me. My mother was preoccupied with the dress I was to wear, and after many visits to the dressmaker in Pest, a white wool dress with pink velvet ribbon trim was created. I don't remember much about the confirmation. The church was simple and white-washed and had no angels and I was most aware of my mother sitting behind me watching my performance. I desperately hoped that I would not muff my lines and I stood as straight and tall as I had been told a thousand times. No one asked me to believe in God and in fact no one ever talked to me about my innermost thoughts or concerns. My thoughts were my own and they were off limits to anyone else. Both my parents and the communist world asked that I behave properly; they did not ask to see my thoughts. Inside my own mind I felt free.

The principal did call me and my mother in afterwards. In the office I admitted that I had been confirmed in the Hungarian Reformed Church and that my parents gave me a choice in the matter and I chose to do it on my own. The principal explained that religion was against the spirit of the communist state and if I kept on like this I would not get into the university or might get into deeper trouble. However, I was still young and I could mend my ways with the help of the teachers. For the moment my only punishment was that I would have to give up being the president of the class. The police chief's daughter was made the president of the class. I emerged from the principal's office covered in glory in the eyes of my classmates.

In a complicated world like this, escape into other worlds was attractive and reading made it possible. One of my two favorite books was called *Wonderful Journey* by the Swedish author Selma Lagerlöf. Written at the turn of the century, the book was a children's classic. It was the story of a little boy who had been bad and was turning into a Tom Thumb by magic. Being so tiny he ended up flying with the wild geese on their annual migration on the back of a gray goose. On this trip they had many fantastic adventures, eluding a fox and visiting exotic places even under water. At the end of it the little boy became good and was turned back into a regular size boy only a year older. But as a regular boy he no longer understood the language of the animals and could no longer fly with the wild geese. Tears came to my eyes as I read about the tears described in the boy's eyes at this tremendous loss. The ending of the book always made me cry. (I recently found this book in English entitled *The Wonderful Adventures of Nils*, and learned that the geese actually fly all over Sweden and it was sort of a geography lesson. My Hungarian version was less specifically Swedish and more universal.)

In my second favorite book the heroine doesn't go home at all. The fairy Szille lives with her father, the King of the Lakes, who has forbidden her to leave her home, but with the help of a fish she goes out in the outer world. This outer world is inhabited by birds and animals who quarrel and have adventures. Szille becomes queen of this world and lives there happily every after. The fish tries hopelessly to find the way back but can't in any case (*The Book of the Lakes* [Tavak Könyve], Albert Wass, 1943). This book was illustrated with some light line drawings of Szille in her watery world. The book was miraculously saved by Uncle Feri who came to get our things after 1956 and gave it back to me on a visit in the 1980's. I was astonished to discover that the ancient American mural I was writing about for my dissertation had a similar scene of a woman with open arms in a watery natural setting as in one of the illustrations. Like many Hungarian books, for example, *Be Faithful Unto Death*, Hungarian books for children were often sad or melancholy. Szille's story started out with a sad God creating the world and ended with a remedy for sadness:

Because you too will be sad in life. Life holds sadnesses for everyone. And if you now and then become sad and walk up and down uselessly among people and you feel that no one helps with your great sadness...one night steal down to the lake. Close your eyes. And all at once you will see the dance of the birds in the shallows. And then, on that quiet night the lake itself will tell you a story, continuing where I left off. And on that quiet night you will forget, for sure, that you were sad.

Actually, Szille's story wasn't all that sad – she had become queen of her world.

Perhaps at thirteen I was coming to develop an independent self away from my parents and had fantasies of journeys that the escape from Hungary made all too real. I was still treated as a little girl and in Hungary children became young adults without the long and complicated adolescence of Americans. Although I played with dolls still, hormones were beginning to direct my attention to romance. For my tenth Christmas I received a set of the collected plays of Shakespeare in Hungarian, divided into Tragedies, Comedies, and Histories. I devoured the comedies, gaining half my sexual education and notion of the relationship between the sexes from them. The other half of my romantic knowledge came from reading *Gone with the Wind*, a book I discovered on my parent's bookshelf, also in Hungarian. This book was censured by the communists because it was felt that the struggle of the American South against the North in the Civil War would be interpreted as the struggle of Hungary against the Soviets. Books were dangerous because everyone interpreted them metaphorically. My mother forbade the book as "too grown up sexually" and therefore inappropriate. I read the book in sections, sneaking it in and out of the bookshelf by way of the jingling crystal bar cart. I skipped the war chapters because I knew nothing about the Civil War nor where Atlanta was and at that point its burning didn't mean much to me. I was interested in Scarlett's feelings for Ashley and Rhett and I cried when Rhett didn't give a damn. I didn't want an unhappy ending; in my mind the lovers were subsequently united.

Closer to home, I was developing a crush on the tall, handsome man who lived across the street, the owner of the other car. It didn't bother me that he was my father's age and similarly bald. He was the glamorous director and stage and costume designer of the opera house.

He gave us girls tickets to Mozart's "Magic Flute" and "Don Giovanni" which were probably the highlights of my childhood. When he came for dinner he brought us chocolates and dolls. After seeing the operas I spent my time designing costumed for the characters of the Queen of the Night, Pamela, Donna Anna, Donna Elvira and Zerlina – all the female leads, which were of course similar to the ones I had seen. We put a blanket over the table in our room and enacted puppet theaters of the operas, fairy tales, the stories from history with our dolls. I fell in love with the handsome baritone singing Don Giovanni's champagne aria, all dressed up in white, but this was just a passing fancy because I never saw him again. The real love was Guszti Olah, the neighbor we could spy on, and run away, giggling, if we saw him. I wouldn't know for many years that Guszti Oláh was single because he was a homosexual nor what a homosexual was. He also left the country in 1956. We thought he brought us candy because he was in love with us. In leaving Hungary I didn't know that I would be leaving my childhood behind at the same moment.

4
Progressive Teen

Kukachin: "Say this, I loved and died. Now I am love and live."
Marco Millions, Eugene O'Neil, 1923

At the age of fifteen I had the leading role of Kukachin in a play by Eugene O'Neil at the Cambridge School of Weston, a coeducational progressive school outside Boston. Less than a year and half before I did not speak a word of English and I am sure I had then, as I still do now, an accent. To this day I remember most of the lines and my intonations and that of the others in the cast; I was Kukachin then and perhaps I still am. This is one of Eugene O'Neil's least known and admired plays. It is about a Chinese princess whose father is the great Kublai Khan who is taken to be married by a very appropriate Persian prince by the Venetian merchant Marco Polo on the way back to Europe. She falls desperately in love with Marco, but all Marco is interested in is money; he keeps talking about "millions" and does not see her superior poetic soul. When she gets to Persia she dies of unrequited love and her body is carried back to the khan in a coffin. There her otherworldly voice says to the terrified carriers: "Say this, I loved and died. Now I am love and live." Marco gets back to Venice to marry his old and fat sweetheart and live on his money.

So I was to be this ethereal Chinese princess, a role for which I was much too tall but perhaps had the requisite foreign accent and exotic high cheekbones. Kukachin spoke mainly in poetry and as I revisited the play recently I was amazed how the feelings she expresses must have matched my own those days about having left Hungary. This is part of her poem to her father:

> My heart is bitter and tears blur my eyes.
> I grieve for the days when we lingered together
> In the spring we sang of love and laughed with youth
> But now we are parted by many leagues and years
> And I weep that never again shall I see your face.

Being the lead in this play, so soon, in a resplendent Chinese gown and shiny headdress I found myself the center of school and it remains one of the most exciting moments of my life. As I was writing these lines it occurred to me for the first time that perhaps it was not accidental. The Cambridge School had a wonderful drama program, putting on one major play, and a senior play, each year by the unforgettable drama coach Whitney Haley who with a booming voice acted out every part for us to imitate. (He was hilarious in women's parts.) Plays were the usual Gilbert and Sullivan operettas and comedies like *The Importance of Being Ernest*. It has occurred to me now that Whitney Haley chose *Marco Millions* with me in mind from the beginning to work with me, to help me, to show me off – for many possible reasons.

The Cambridge School was a small place – there were only about two hundred boarding students so we all knew each other by name. I was very lucky because it was one of the freest and yet most sheltering places I have ever encountered. I spent some of the happiest years of my life there. When I arrived in January 1957 I came as a celebrity – local newspapers published my photograph and announced my presence. On many occasions I had to stand up and acknowledge clapping, and smiled in return, since I spoke no English as yet. I was representing the "freedom fighters." Generally I felt great sympathy and approval towards me. That meant a great deal since for the first time I was alone and in a foreign country. My success or failure depended on my wits.

The first evening when I got to the dorm, known as White Farm House, the girls took me to the common room and gave me a snack – peanut butter spread on saltines and a glass of milk. I had never had peanut butter before and the stuff stuck to the roof of my mouth and I was in a panic because I was unable to dislodge it, to spit it out and it felt like my mouth would be permanently glued together. I couldn't decide if it was meant to be sweet or salty. Tears almost came to my eyes at this unclassifiable stuff in my mouth. I knew that the girls gave me this out of kindness and eventually got it down. Having my mouth glued together panicked me because I was speechless as is.

Even though I understood not a word, I went to classes and let the English words fall on me like a waterfall, hoping that something would stick. I went to French class and I could speak to a few students who took French III and Madame Washburn took me under her wing. But the best time I had in those speechless days was in the art studio. I spent as much time as I could painting this and that. For example, I set up bottles and still life arrangements and painted them with light and shade in the academic tradition, as I had been taught in Hungary. (We had art classes there, too.) I had learned how to measure proportion with a pencil. This impressed my fellow students who had never done anything like this. I was greatly helped and welcomed by Althea Carr who ran the art studio. After a while, however, she and the other teachers seemed to feel that I was not going in the right direction with art. They were trying to get me to do different things. For example, they showed me how to tear up bits of colorful paper and glue them back on a sheet helter-skelter, which they called a collage. I tried to do this but for the life of me I could not figure out what was achieved by pushing bits of paper hither and yon making patterns that were sometimes nice, sometimes confusing and meaningless. I did gather that they were trying to "free me up" but they didn't seem to realize that I had been "freed up" of practically everything in my life.

I went from being a little girl who played with dolls in November 1956 to a teen who aroused boys in January 1957. I was a sensation among the boys the first day in the dining room in a sweater without a bra. In the afternoon the girls took me immediately to Woolworth's to buy me a bra and confine my breasts. In Hungary since I was technically a little girl I wouldn't wear a grown up item like a bra for some time. No one worried about budding breasts. As a little in girl in Hungary I was supposed to wear short skirts above the knees. But this was America in the 1950's and girls wore skirts down to their ankles. It was confusing. When I first went home on vacation I took off the bra in the train bathroom so my mother would not think that I was trying to be more grown up than I was. She bought me short skirts and I wore them out of loyalty. American above the waist – Hungarian below.

The visit home for the first time in New York that first March vacation was an eye-opener. The furnished room in the sickly shades of green was clearly not big enough for the two daughters. My parents moved to better quarters eventually, but I never had a room or space in my parents' apartments. They somehow seemed to feel that already I really lived elsewhere. My parents looked shabby, exhausted and lost among all the big buildings. In two months I knew more English and more about America than they did. I loved them, I clung to them, but they could not help me here. That's when I felt really alone, surrounded by strangers in a strange world. School was my home now and I gave myself up to it and my schoolmates became my world.

The girls took me in hand: they shaved my legs and armpits; I seemed "primitive" to them and they "civilized" me. I let them reshape me passively. It somehow seemed right, all this preoccupation with the body – my remaking began with my body which had to be initiated into American forms and customs. Unfortunately, nothing could be done about my name. Miskolczy is unpronounceable in America. The name means "from the town of Miskolc" which is, of course, not where my family comes from. The "czy" is an upper class ending meaning "from" and if my father had had social pretension he might have changed it to "de Miskolc" or "von Miskolc" but thank god he did no such thing. Many refugees "translated" their names through such verbal ennoblement. Egalitarian Americans loved European nobility. But Miskolczy was unpronounceable in America, every consonant in the alphabet seemed to get between the M and the Y. In college a few clever professors called me "Miss Kolsky." Some gave up and called me "Miss M." Marriage gave me the easier Pasztory that was pronounceable Italian style.

Not that in those days I was thinking of marriage. I was still thinking about my dolls which I knew better than to mention. Here the girls my age were thinking about their boyfriends. They danced with boys either wiggling madly or glued to each other. They danced to someone called Elvis Presley or Johnny Mathis which was loud and as meaningless to me as moving colored pieces of paper around to make a picture. I had been raised on Mozart and Beethoven and dancing to me meant the Viennese waltz, the tango or the czardas as I learned them from my father. If all their stories about the West were true, those Cambridge Schoolers should have been dancing the waltz and the tango in elegant dress. Instead, the girls wore oversized men's shirts over their jeans and gyrated to Elvis. I escaped to my European cultural superiority, trying to pretend that that noise did not exist. I was amazed, however, to discover decades later that I remembered every word of those hated songs with great nostalgia because in the end, like it or not, that was my youth. A song like "See the pyramids, along the Nile…" can make it all come back. At the time, however, it was all so alien I might as well have landed on Mars.

Cut off from my family and friends like Edda, I was lonely a great deal. I tried to make friends with some of the girls but until Ann Robbins in the later years, these friendships were not very serious. I tried to hold hands with my first roommate, the way girls held hands in Hungary as a matter of course, but she drew back as if a viper had bit her. I felt rejected. Later on I learned that this was considered lesbian behavior and that girls must not be touched. Evidently touching was all right only with boys. Not surprisingly when I was fourteen, my second year there, I had found a boyfriend. David was from South America and probably as lonely for home as I. Our romance consisted of long walks on the trails in the woods and fields surrounding the school buildings and holding hands. When in the course of time he finally tried to kiss me, I did what my mother had told me to do. She said: "If any male tries to kiss you, give them a slap (*pofon*)." So I gave him a resounding "pofon" which surprised him and was the talk of the boys' dormitory. Something was wrong with my education as far as boys were concerned. Actually we remained friends and our picture is in the yearbook at the prom looking happy. David did not come back to school the following year and I do not know what happened to him.

My sex education couldn't have been more limited. My godmother told my mother in Hungary that she did not have to bother with the birds and the bees talk, because she would do the educating. This consisted of taking me to an Italian grimly realistic (*verismo*) movie in black and white in which the young girl fell in love with somebody, got pregnant out of wedlock, and drowned herself in a lake. I was dizzy when we came out of the movie theater. That lesson was very clear: "Don't get pregnant and wait until marriage to have sex otherwise terrible things will happen." These dire warnings came before I had any idea of how you actually get pregnant.

There were other possible terrible fates. Next to Dracula the other Hungarians mentioned by well-meaning Americans when we first came were the Gabor sisters: Zsazsa, Eva, Magda and their mother Jolie who had come out in the late Forties. They were better known than Albert Szent-Györgyi and his Nobel Prize! Eva and Zsazsa appeared on TV with their bleached blonde hair and heavy make-up, flaunting their sexuality, marriages, and yes, their Hungarian accents. I never heard their names referred to in Hungary but they were celebrities in America. When the Gabor sisters were first mentioned to my mother, her reaction was horror and a sense of insult that they should be mentioned in her company at all. She described how she had seen them in the lobby of the Kékes resort hotel my father built before the war with Mama Gabor urging her daughters to pull their skirts higher and reveal more leg for the prospective rich foreign customers. In my mother's eyes, the Gabor women were expensive call girls and all their talk of diamonds was the height of vulgarity. But that is not how the Americans viewed them; they seemed to see them as plucky Europeans who had made good careers for themselves as celebrities and more power to them. The awful thing was that Americans thought they were typical Hungarians and we could not talk them out of that idea. The Gabor sisters came to play a strangely important role in my life in America – practically like invisible relatives, they were constantly brought up as examples of what not to do. Their "careers" were not to be imitated, but of course their success was. In the end, my mother succumbed to the fascination with the Gabor sisters and with us and other Hungarians they were a common and endless topic of conversation. A lot of hilarity focused on the "freedom fighter" Zsazsa married for a while after 1956 who claimed to be a count, but of course wasn't. Hungarians called him "Count Kilmer" after the New Jersey army base where all Hungarian refugees arrived and readjusted their identity. The Gabors were, however, ostentatiously *not* invited to important social functions like the annual Hungarian ball at the Plaza which they could have bought with one of their rings.

Once I was away at boarding school my parents seem to have lost a sense of who I was and how old I was. Sometimes they treated me as a little girl and my mother sent me shoeboxes full of cookies that usually arrived as crumbs. Sometimes they saw me as a grown up because I took the train and came and went by myself. I was tall and looked more like nineteen than fourteen or fifteen. The cookie package might be followed by a full-length fake chinchilla coat to keep me warm in the New England winter. She probably got it for pennies at some thrift shop. I actually wore it and some of my friends created a "happening" around me in that coat that amused everybody. Sometimes my parents seemed to want to marry me off right then and there. My mother sometimes lent me her low-cut cocktail dresses and jewelry and sent me out with some "trusted" male friend of the family in his thirties. I remember once going to the Latin Quarter night club with a girlie show and dancing cheek to cheek with a fat young doctor smelling of aftershave. I suppose that was to give me some experience of the world. I was expected to marry someone older and to remain a virgin until the wedding. It was all terribly confusing. My life at school and my visits home were practically on separate planets.

The strangest discovery I made in school was that I was experienced as a tabula rasa, an empty self, to be filled in the by the new American culture. Once I learned English I found that everyone was interested in my escape story, knew a few facts about the Hungarian revolution but no one knew anything about Hungary and no one was interested in knowing anything. They didn't know where Hungary was geographically, they assumed I spoke a Slavic language (no!), and except for the Russian-Eastern European conflict they saw no differences between any of those people. This was a very painful revelation: Hungary did not matter to them at all. Americans have never heard of the poet Petőfi or any of the stories and heroes I grew up with. My whole childhood was meaningless here. I discovered that Hungary as a culture simply did not exist in the new world. I might as well have dropped in from another planet. I was experienced as a handsome body, with no known culture, to be easily Americanized. From what I could observe, I liked America and wanted to be Americanized. Nevertheless I made a personal vow never to forget my own past, to pass on my non-Indo-European language and culture to my children when I had them, and to marry only a Hungarian. And I fulfilled that vow, though in real life things were not so simple. My parents were totally unaware of these conflicts nor would I have had the ability to express them then.

Complexity came in the form of a boy who came up to me at some music recital at the Cambridge School when I was fifteen or sixteen and started to talk to me about Hungarian history and asked me questions about the first communists revolution of 1919 by Béla Kun. He was the first American to treat me as a person with a history. I actually didn't know much about Béla Kun, but it turned out that he was well versed in Hungarian history and literature. I was quite captivated by Marc. Many years later he told me that he wanted to get to know me and read up on these subjects in the library. He had read up on many other subjects too and seemed to have a brilliant and encyclopaedic mind. For much of the first part of my life Marc Haefele was my guide to the puzzle and mystery of American life. Girls asked me what I saw in him because he was cross-eyed (later corrected) and teachers told me that he was not appropriate for me, but I paid them no heed. Considering his mind, Marc did not do well and was an unconventional student who flaunted his unconventionality. He had a full length black cape made and walked around in it on campus instead of a coat, a veritable Dracula. But Marc knew things and understood things and we became a couple roaming the fields and paths. I held to my insistence on remaining a virgin and he respected that. There was no way to explain much of what happened at the Cambridge School to my parents and certainly no way to explain Marc. And so I didn't.

Marc's parents lived in Florida at the time and I imagined that he was "southern" in the sense of *Gone with the Wind* and that appealed to me. But he wasn't southern, he came from the Midwest and in American fashion, his parents lived in various places for a time. His father had a position in banking but they were not particularly wealthy or intellectual. They didn't quite know what to do with their extraordinary son. Moreover, they were Christian Scientists, hence the delay in fixing the eyes. I was totally confused by all the different religious denominations in the US and nothing was more confusing than Christian Science to someone with doctors in the family. Marc was the first American I got to know really well and to my European eyes he and his family seemed to be a mass of contradictions between very progressive and very backward elements. I had never met anyone like him and for a long time I thought that he was a "typical" American. I had finally met my American.

I had no pocket money; my allowance of about $2 a month was just about enough to keep me in the novelty of the potato chips I loved. The girls often ordered pizza or Chinese food and invited me to partake knowing that I could not reciprocate. They took me to the movies. I learned how to accept charity. Marc had an allowance sufficient to take me to concerts and inexpensive French restaurants in addition to pizza. He introduced me to cool jazz and beat poetry. He had friends who shared some "beatnik" features, but he himself was too idiosyncratic to belong to any group. It's just that these people, including the composers

George Edwards and Pril Smiley, were the most intelligent and interested in intellectual things. I was not suited to the cheerleader and football player crowd. On weekends Marc and I went into Boston to see museums such as the Gardner Museum which was our favorite. The Gardner Museum looked like a pirate's treasure trove of art – the most unlikely furniture, paintings and sculptures were brought together in profusion from all over the world. Isabella Gardner seemed to have been a lady who didn't much care for society's "good taste" and seemed to like all sorts of oddities. I sensed in her a vitality similar to the maid's silk dress with big red tulips that broke the code of propriety my parents brought me up with. This was the America I fell in love with.

We also went to see movies at the Brattle Theater in Cambridge where I was most impressed by Jean Cocteau's *Orfée*. I didn't really need the English subtitles. The story is a modern version of the Greek myth in which the disconsolate Orpheus whose wife died goes down to the underworld to get her back. He can get her and take her back so long as he does not look at her on the long journey. He of course eventually looks back and loses her forever. In the Jean Cocteau version I was most taken by the figure of Death played by a very beautiful Maria Casarez in a spectacular black gown that sometimes looked white. Brutal motorcyclists actually caused or were present at the deaths. People moved from one world to the other through mirrors which parted like water. I think Death had a soft spot for Orfée and there was a suggestion that the motorcyclists would take her away and something namelessly awful might happen to her. She reminded me of the Queen of the Night in Mozart's "Magic Flute" and the melodramatic story of two worlds, deaths, loves, and pride appealed to my teenage soul which was not at ease despite successful outward appearances. Marc supplied the companionship, the know-how in getting around and what to see, and the funds to do it with. Without him my time at the Cambridge School would have been much more limited and much less exciting. Although I was deeply attached to him, I tried to indicate that we didn't have much of a future, since he was just a boy and I had something else in mind in a husband. All that however was so far away that we simply indulged in each other's company.

My senior year was a year of fulfillment. I was rooming with Ann Robbins, a shy little blond girl who fitted in well with my own little girlish shyness. We made colorful charts depicting the life-cycles of seeds and animals for the walls of the biology lab until late at night. I visited her parents in Rochester and took driving lessons there so I could get my license. At school I was voted president of the Town Meeting – a meeting of all students, faculty, and staff – and the accolade was marvelous but I did not know what to do with the position and was greatly relieved when it was over. I have no political talents. The Shakespeare play selected for the senior class was *The Tempest* and I was chosen to play Miranda, the daughter of Prospero the magician. The lithe Ann Robbins played the spirit Ariel and Marc played Trinculo, a jester. We were all in it together. The play is about shipwrecked Prospero and Miranda on an enchanted island meeting up with the villains who caused their troubles in the first place. Prospero and Ariel do some tricks and everything works out. Miranda weds the right young nobleman and they go home happily. The part of Miranda was not as exciting as Kukachin; she was just your typical young heroine who was married off, but it was the leading female role and I got to say those classic lines that meant a great deal to me personally:

> O, wonder,
> How many goodly creatures are there here!
> How beauteous mankind is! O brave new world
> That hath such people in it!

Considering the richness, adventure, and excitement of the time at the Cambridge School my summers at home were tame. The first summer in New York, unprepared for the heat and without air-conditioning, my mother and us girls spent our time in stores although we had no money to spend or in museums where we could spend hours in coolness for free. Our favorite was the Frick Collection which was like being a private house with beautiful paintings. I knew where every painting was and still mind when they move things around. Another favorite spot was Radio City Music Hall where for 99 cents (if you went at noon) you could stay for the movie and the show which lasted more than four hours. For a while I was plucked from this routine by Ellen Harrison, the wife of my father's employer, Wallace Harrison. She wanted to do something for us and it was evident that she couldn't do anything with my mother because my mother considered herself to be her social equal and would not be patronized. But maybe something could be done with me. She invited me to their house on Long Island, ostensibly to catalogue their library, as a summer job and paid me something. (Americans do not like young people to be jobless in the summer.) The Long Island estate consisted of a not very memorable contemporary architecture designed by Harrison and included a large round swimming pool with a Leger painting on its bottom. That was memorable. Leger supplied the sketch and workmen did the rest. This went with the Calder mobiles and other modern art also in their New York apartment on Fifth Avenue. (The Fifth Avenue apartment had a life size copy of Picasso's Guernica in tapestry in the dining room.) The Harrisons lived in their own Museum of Modern Art and were supporters of the Museum itself. I got some information on the Dewey Decimal System and reorganized the library, which was much smaller than the one I have now, and it was unlikely that the Harrisons would put their books back according to the numbers I was putting on them. Moreover it seemed that someone had done this before – many books had numbers that I had to cover over to put mine on. So, the Harrisons were eccentric rich folks and that was fine with me. I got to have couple of weeks away from the heat of the city. This was also the time that I discovered their catalogues from the Museum of Primitive Art, founded by Rockefeller, with images of the strangest and most interesting sculptures. I found them more interesting than the modern art in the Harrisons' house. Mrs. Harrison treated me sometimes as an employee and sometimes as a relative – perhaps a poor relation. She gave me hand-me-down clothes, which included one spectacular Paris original full length black evening coat that came in handy for many Hungarian balls later. She was very nice to me and introduced me to other members of the family including a young man who wanted to take me out. I don't remember the name of the young man, but he was nice and polite but as soon as it appeared that he might like me for real, he disappeared. This was the family of the Rockefellers – Ellen was a Milton and a close relation of Nelson Rockefeller. They did not want any fortune-hunting Hungarian girls near their young men. So after this initial interest the Harrisons went back to their world and I to whatever was mine.

My summer world was Lake Owassa in New Jersey. Finding the hot and humid New York summer unbearable, my father looked for a summer place to rent and through an ad found a Viennese doctor who rented his cottage in New Jersey for July and August while he went to Vienna. They could afford to rent it because another couple joined them. The Szántos were among the people they met in Vienna and they too came to the US and to New York. The Owassa place was just right for two families in that there was separate apartment over the garage. The main house was simple, with fabric curtains tacked up to separate the rooms. But it was water-front with a very wide deck, a large gazebo and a barbecue pit. Except for one disastrous summer we spent in Lenox, I spent every summer here until 1970. The only drawback of the place was that in the later years the water became green from eutrification, common then in those lakes, and was not appetizing to swim in. Otherwise we might eventually have looked for a place to buy there.

Most of the time everyone at our place at Lake Owassa was Hungarian. On weekends we had guests such as the Pinters, the sister of Mrs. Szánto and her husband. We would swim and sun ourselves on the deck, have a chicken or pork barbecue with our special paprika and wine sauce. As it got dark we'd move the table in the gazebo to one side and dance old-fashioned dances like the tango and sing along to popular Hungarian songs from the early 1950's like "You are the light in the night, the white ship on the ocean…. (Te vagy a fény az éjszakában, Tenger vizén fehér hajó…). It was all in Hungarian, exiles bemoaning the old country, happy to be barbecuing in the new. Kristina and I were treated as children again and it was an adult world. My father was the ruler of the Owassa kingdom.

During the week all the adults went back to New York to work and we stayed with my mother, without a car. If we needed anything my sister and I would canoe across the lake where there was a little store. Mrs. Harrison had urged that we should have summer jobs like camp counselors but my father would not have it. He believed in play for young people. I spent my time reading books that I had brought or found in the Viennese doctor's bookshelf. I helped my mother cook and learned basic Hungarian cooking. I daydreamed. I started novels I never finished. After dinner we played dominoes and Monopoly. Occasionally I got an amazing letter from Marc in a wild, modernistic, stream of consciousness style in which he said he would not sign "love" for fear of my parents finding out and hid the word backward inside other words such as "evolution" and "revolution." I was impressed and imagined that no other young woman had ever received such love letters.

That one summer in Lenox was on the advice of an American couple, friends of Kristina's from Windsor Mountain School. It was expensive because Lenox is an elegant summer place. We had a small house nowhere near water and the country club would not have us. The lingerie business begun by my mother and Edna from a room in the local hotel failed miserably. Next summer we went back to Lake Owassa with the Szántos and we kept going there until my sister and I were married and bought our own places and the Szántos and the Pinters acquired their own far enough away so we rarely saw each other. The refugee extended "family," or in later parlance "commune," disappeared.

My parents wanted me to come closer to New York and after the years at the Cambridge School I was nostalgic for home. My sister, who was only eleven when she went there, did not get along well at the Windsor Mountain School and came home to live in New York and went to a nearby school. As good as I was academically, I could have gone to Radcliffe but did not apply in order not to go so far from my parents. Of the schools near New York City, Vassar gave me a scholarship and I went there in order to be close to home. I hated Vassar. I hated being in an all-female environment. It was a big place and for the first time I felt that many girls were rich and I was poor. At the Cambridge School I never felt poor. Poughkeepsie was a dump with none of the amenities of Boston. The most you could do in Poughkeepsie was have pizza. I went on mixers to meet boys at Princeton and other places which were humiliating experiences. I never met anybody.

My parents seemed to think that college was the equivalent of a European university and kept asking me what "profession" I had chosen. I had no idea. After my theatrical successes I thought of becoming an actress, so one day in New York I went to see a director who had placed an ad in the newspaper. I wore my mother's wraparound coat to look more sophisticated. The man had me read something and then he put an arm around my waist, probably meaning nothing. I ran out in a panic and that was the end of my theatrical career. My father wanted to know if I wanted to be an architect or a doctor. I was interested in architecture, but in the same breath he told me that women have a hard time dealing with contractors and talked me out of it. So to placate everybody I announced that I wanted to be a stage and costume designer like Guszti Oláh, which seemed reasonable and acceptable and appropriate to a woman. My father advised that in order to do so I should take an art history course and learn all the different styles. That's how I got to art history. Vassar had a wonderful art history introductory course and I was fascinated by the intellectual aspect of it. I abandoned the idea of stage and costume design and began to ask who did what, where, and why – questions I still ask today. I wasn't so much anxious to make things, I wanted explanations as to why things are the way they are. Of the few friends I made there, Jane Gregory was one who was interested in the same questions and made me feel that I wasn't barking up the wrong tree.

I met Blaise Pasztory (Blaise is "Balázs" in Hungarian) at some event in Hungarian society, but then we were formally introduced at a lunch by a rather dissolute old Hungarian who ran a card club. A dance was coming up in the early summer at the Tavern on the Green in Central Park and he thought Blaise would make a good partner for me. The lunch was made less awkward by the fact that the old guy got drunk at the table and the two of us laughed at the ridiculous situation and began to talk to each other. We discovered in just a few minutes that our histories were very similar. He came out of Hungary in 1948 at the age of eleven with his mother who had a grant at the Institute for Advanced Studies at Princeton in art history. She specialized in the Renaissance. He was sent to boarding schools, Eaglebrook School when small and Exeter later, and then went to Harvard and Harvard Law. He was now working in a law firm. I had a similarly stellar school experience. But then we also had our hungarianness in common and talked in Hungarian to each other. We understood the nature of the older generation of Hungarians, we understood something about Americans. We also understood that hungarianness was important to both of us. While we did not understand each other personally very deeply, we understood fully our circumstances and that was very exciting. There were not many people our age in the Hungarian community because many who left in 1956 were in their twenties and few people came with children. It was unlikely that I'd meet another person like Blaise. We went to the dance, which was held outdoors under the stars and had a magical time. It was my first dance in formal dress with ballroom dancing and I loved every minute of it. In a few weeks Blaise visited me at Lake Owassa and on a walk in the woods proposed. I though that he must be kidding. I was only eighteen years old, a freshman in college and had no thought about marriage in the immediate future. I wanted to finish college.

I agonized whether to marry him for almost six months. I was still seeing Marc, who was at New York University, and in time both men knew that I was trying decide which one to take. I was very close to Marc, we had a long history together, I was terrified that if I left him he'd fall apart or even that I'd fall apart. But Marc was a kid like me and in no position to marry anyone. If anything, his mind was on the acquisition of a motorcycle – a perfectly reasonable quest for a young American male. But I was an immigrant who slept on the bottom part of a trundle bed in my sister's room when I came home and I needed a home now and not far off in the future. The motorcycle irritated me. Blaise was my parents' idea of an ideal husband for me: he had a job and a salary and we could have a home – not only a home, but a Hungarian home in the midst of the New York Hungarian community. I was starved for my Hungarian heritage. I agonized for months because I loved Marc. I agreed to spend New Year's Eve with both of them, which was an impossibility. In the end I broke up with Marc and cried for days. Later in the winter my sister and I were "presented" at the Hungarian ball at the Plaza, another formal occasion, and in the summer of 1963 Blaise and I were married in the Hungarian Reformed Church on East 82nd Street. I transferred to Barnard and we had a small apartment in the East Eighties. That was the first home I had in the US.

This agonized decision between Marc and Blaise was not merely a matter of the persons involved, although at the time I saw it like that. It was the beginning of a dilemma that has haunted me my whole adult life: am I Hungarian or American? I enjoyed the Cambridge School as an innocent exploring another culture, but then both that America and my mother culture laid claim on me with equal force in the form of Marc and Blaise. On the one hand I tried to be totally American, and then my Hungarian self howled in pain; on the other hand when I chose Hungary I missed America. At age twenty I had no way of combining the two and perhaps I still don't. I chose to go home. I could not go home to Budapest so the second best was to go home to the exile community in New York. But in choosing the exile community I cut off everything the Cambridge School stood for and that was very difficult. A lot of this agonizing I wrote in my diary which I had kept at school almost since my arrival. Before the wedding I threw it down my parents' incinerator and burned it. I didn't want Blaise to see it and I was starting a new life, cutting off the past. (I'd give anything to have it back with those first observations.)

5
Ancient America

"What's a nice girl like you doing studying Aztec Art?"

This was usually asked at conferences by older men, implying that I had kinky tastes and they were curious as to what they might be. The Aztecs have the reputation of being one of the most horrible people on earth and I had just written the first book on Aztec art. I never knew what to answer and usually mumbled something about their beautiful art and profound poetry. Faced with the Aztecs, however, all anyone can think of is the large number of sacrificial victims who had their hearts cut out. The question required a short answer and I could not explain that though the Aztecs indeed sacrificed many victims, in actual fact their atrocities and body counts on the battlefield were quite limited because they fought a kind of ceremonial battle in which they tried to take prisoners alive and did not kill on the battlefield. Figured that way they were less brutal than the Spanish Conquistadors who shot to kill on the field, than the Inquisition that was instituted shortly after the conquest and, going further afield, the Romans, the Tartars, the Mongols, the First World War, the Nazis, the Communists, Hiroshima and Nagasaki, 9/11, and perhaps throwing in the headhunters of New Guinea and South America. We are a violent species but we accept horrendous casualties in war as justifiable.

We are, however, squeamish about the human sacrifices all ancient people performed from South America to China. One difference is that in the case of the Aztecs we have detailed and extensive reports by Christian missionaries to horrify and/or secretly titillate. I have always been more interested in understanding than in condemning the practice. Considering that most people are reasonably rational and often humane, why is this practice world wide? I don't know the answer completely but I see some aspects of it. Ancient cultures saw themselves as an integral part of nature and felt they needed to reciprocate the bounty and avoid the wrath nature could produce. (We think that nature is inanimate or dead and master it scientifically.) As ancient people fed on nature they imagined that nature needed to feed on something equally precious to keep producing. Nature was fed by death, as dust turned into dust, but needed more in the form of blood. The Aztecs believed that their world was soon to end, with the end of the gods as well, and tried to convince the powers that be to keep going by sacrifices. Their sacrifices were especially bloody because they tried to show nature and their constituents that they were doing everything they could in a very visible way. To me the Aztecs were just like any other ancient people such as the Assyrians or the ancient Chinese who practiced various forms of violence.

It's not that I liked the sacrifices, mostly I disregarded them as the distasteful violence one might find in any society. Besides, I grew up in a world in which violence was in the open and not hidden and in some ways it had the virtue of being visible. Even we schoolchildren had our childish "violence" in that we played practical jokes on our teachers that sometimes could have ended in injury and were severely punished for them; taking the punishment well was a matter of honor. But tricks and practical jokes were expected of children in Hungary. At the Cambridge School such tricks would have been seen as very strange and "sick." The faculty were supposed to be "friends" and not targets even though they had the power to punish or kick you out of school if you misbehaved. Power relations were played down and at first I found that very unusual. The Aztecs wanted to play up power relations and I did not find that surprising. Secondly, while not in the same grisly manner, we grew up on the idea of "sacrifice" for the greater good. Violence bred resistance and sacrifice. Our poet Petőfi "sacrificed himself" for the revolution of 1848, Count Teleki sacrificed himself for the honor of Hungary in 1944, and I am sure most of my class would have sacrificed themselves at Eger castle in the battle against the Turks. That explains the twelve and fourteen year old children who fought and often died in the 1956 revolution.

There is one particular Aztec story that rang a bell with the sacrificial ideas I grew up with. A foreign Aztec lord was captured in battle and was to be sacrificed by being tied to a stone and given useless implements. Four fully armed jaguar warriors engaged him in gladiatorial combat, one after the other. The custom was that if he survived the ordeal, he could go free. This particular lord survived the ordeal showing exceptional bravery and was set free. He went away and lived with his family for a whole year. After a year he came back and offered himself for sacrifice; he felt that he had cheated the gods and owed to them his life. This story may be true or it may have been reformulated to fit the Aztec ideal. Very likely such stories were told to young boys to make them brave. All I'm saying is that you didn't have to be an Aztec to be brought up on stories of sacrifice.

The same people who are known world-wide as brutal sacrificers wrote some of the most beautiful poetry which is much less known. The poems were written by rulers, aristocratic men and bards, and were recited at feasts. The sixteenth century Spanish wrote them down in the Aztec language. Many are about the nature of life and death and express Aztec feelings and concerns. Here are two of my favorites:

Remove trouble from your hearts, oh my friends.
As I know, so do others;
Only once do we live.
Let us in peace and pleasure spend our lives;
Come, let us enjoy ourselves!
Let not those who live in anger join us.
The earth is so vast.
Oh! that one could live forever!
Oh! that one never had to die!

What are you meditating?
What are you remembering, oh my friends?
Meditate no longer!
At our side the beautiful flowers bloom;
So does the Giver of Life concede pleasure to man.
All of us, if we meditate, if we remember,
Become sad here.

Poetry like that was not written by thugs. The Aztecs were more complicated than we give them credit for.

The question of why I study ancient American art has been asked most frequently in a slightly different form by students and new acquaintances. That conversation goes something like this:

"Which part of Latin America do you come from?"

"None; I come from Hungary."

"Oh." Pause. The person is trying to think where Hungary is.

"So how come you work on ancient American art?" The person can't find an obvious connection between Hungary and ancient America and it seems strange. My usual quick answer is to say that I went to Mexico and saw the marvelous ruins and fell in love with the place and most people find that satisfying because the ruins are spectacular and on some level this is true. But of course I could have found the ruins of Greece or Angkor Wat in the same manner.

Actually I found the Aztecs by a roundabout route. After I transferred to Barnard I decided to follow the interest in art history that I developed at Vassar. I took every course in European art from Egypt to Modern Art. Barnard had a wonderful program and had courses in all kinds of Oriental art and I took those, too. A wonderful southern lady by the name of Jane Mahler taught the art of Islam, Persia, India, China and Japan all in the course of a year. She was not a famous scholar but her enthusiasm was contagious. She wore the most fantastic eastern jewelry and sometimes took off a bracelet and passed it to the class with the instructions of "Feel the jade, people." I was apparently fascinated by the exotic. In an anthropology class we were given the assignment to write about some kind of "primitive" object seen in a museum or gallery.

By "primitive" it was meant small tribal or chiefly cultures in Africa, Australia, New Guinea, New Zealand, Easter Island, and Native Americans like the Iroquois, the Sioux, the Hopi, or the Kwakiutl. These assorted groups, to which Indonesians were sometimes added, had nothing historic in common – they were just similar in being small scale, traditional societies with wonderful woodcarvings, masks, bark paintings, etc. The Museum of Primitive Art was founded in 1957 by Rockefeller to display these magnificent arts. It was located in a townhouse one block from the Museum of Modern Art. "Primitive" objects had come to be considered "art" by artists around 1900 such as Picasso, who were developing more abstract styles and saw them as models and roots. Primitive and Modern were intimately connected. In the 1980's many critics and scholars argued against the term "primitive" as pejorative and insulting to these cultures and it is no longer used. No substitution has been found however and these subjects are no longer connected to each other by a concept. We now speak of the art of Africa, Oceania, Native American Indian quite separately and without relation to one another. The Museum of Primitive Art was folded into the Metropolitan Museum as the "Rockefeller Collection" of African, Oceanic and American art in 1976.

However, when I was at Barnard there was such a thing as "Primitive Art" and I was told to find some and write about it in a paper. I had seen an African art gallery on Lexington Avenue run by someone with an obvious Hungarian name – Ladislaus Segy – and I went there. His gallery was full of strange masks and figures but I was most interested in a group of little brass figurines. Segy explained that these were gold weights from Ghana, made to measure gold dust in the kingdom of the Ashanti. The little figures represented proverbs. I was utterly amazed: gold dust, kingdoms, in sub-Saharan Africa! I had never heard of anything like this. I got books out of the library on the Ashanti and found pictures of impressive kings or chiefs with gold ornaments on their headdresses and sandals, seated on chairs with stools at their feet. They were wearing clothes with geometric designs that turned out to have been woven from silk unraveled from European imports. Sword bearers next to the king augmented his importance in the pictures. I thought I had seen everything in my courses on European and Oriental art, but I never saw anything like this. Then a man came into Segy's shop who turned out to be the famous sculptor Chaim Gross and Segy abandoned me to follow him around with some artifact or other saying in a thick Hungarian accent, "Look, Chaim, how Cubistic!!" To them it was all modern art. After the gold weights I wanted to know what else was there in the world that I knew nothing about.

At Barnard I did not get to know many people and did not live the "college life" because I was married and we were mostly among Hungarian exiles and our relatives. Blaise's father and three grandparents came out from Hungary after 1956. Blaise's father had been crippled in fall in an elevator shaft as he was hiding jewelry belonging to Jews from the Nazis. He was Protestant and as coincidence would have it, his family was from Baja. His wife's father, once an eminent judge, had converted to Christianity from Judaism at the age of eighteen but was nevertheless considered Jewish by the Nazis and had to wear the yellow star. Luckily the whole family was now together. There were also two elderly aunts, daughters of the woman the psychoanalyst Sándor Ferenczi had married. He was not the only noteworthy person in the family in that John von Neumann, the mathematician, game-theorist and partial creator of the atom bomb and computer, was a second cousin. Between Szent Györgyi and von Neumann, we had some of the greatest Hungarian brains of the century in our family. Blaise's relations were then a large extended family of mostly elderly people and they got along with my parents exceedingly well. (Our fathers entertained themselves by remembering old advertising slogans from Baja. "Tagenblatt és Henerári, neked fütyül a kanári." This one loses everything in translation.) My in-laws were intellectually oriented and quite competitive. They were very concerned that I should get all A's and quizzed me about my courses regularly. This was different from my own parents since my father lost interest in my professional future now that I was married and transferred it to Blaise. It didn't matter any more what I would become. I was hurt. My mother merely cautioned against spending too much time in the library and becoming a bluestocking. She advised buying dresses. Blaise was very supportive of whatever direction my interests took. I was blessed.

I just went to Barnard to take the classes and went right home. Other married women were in a similar situation. That's how I became friends with Martha Stewart as we sat together in French class. She was of Polish origin, I was Hungarian. We were both married to lawyers and we socialized at each other's dinner parties for several years afterwards. At that time Martha was a model and a full-page picture of her was often in the *New York Times Magazine*. While I became fascinated with Africa she was interested in the beautiful French castles of the Loire Valley. We were going in different directions.

Blaise urged me to go on to graduate school. His mother had a Ph.D. and he was not intimidated by a woman with a degree. Marriage and family had dulled my ambition and I had no professional vision of what I would do except perhaps teach in secondary school. Blaise argued that if I was to get a Master's it should be in some field and since all I had was art history, it was to be in art history. I decided that I wanted to study those "primitive' cultures I was briefly exposed to. A well-meaning faculty advisor told me that if I went into such an exotic filed I would never get a job and I should think twice about it. However, as Blaise was paying the tuition and I did not have to worry where my next meal came from, I had the luxury of pursuing my interest and not having to trade it in for something more immediately useful. (In those days Columbia, or at least the art history department, did not give fellowships to married women on the grounds that they would have children, leave the field and be a waste of money.)

I entered graduate school at Columbia in 1965 and studied that first year with the elderly Paul Wingert. (The younger member of the faculty, Douglas Fraser, was abroad on sabbatical.) Paul Wingert was famous as the first person who pioneered the study of primitive art in a university – anywhere. When I knew him, a few years before retirement, he was clearly past his prime. He was a short, still shapely person. He was wonderful in many ways but it has to be admitted that he was also very dull in the classroom. One had to be really interested in the material to stick with him. He had a large collection of works of art and he lectured not just with slides but with objects he brought in his briefcase. He described all objects in lengthy, loving detail and explained their uses briefly. Each ethnic group (we then called them tribes) was associated with a style which we learned to recognize and explain. In this manner he slowly and systematically covered the world: the masks and ancestor figures in Africa from Senegal to the Congo. The Maori meeting houses of New Zealand. The rock art of the Australian Aborigines. The shields of New Guinea. The tattooing of Marquesas. The big heads of Easter Island. The False Face masks of the Iroquois. The tipi covers of the Plains. The Hohokam and Anasazi pottery styles of the Southwest. The totem poles of the Kwakiutl. By the end of that first academic year we knew who lived where and when, making what for what purpose, in most of the world and I could go around a museum display naming all the tribal styles of various objects. (I'm still pretty good at it.) Wingert was not much for reading, he was for looking. Mainly he cautioned us against reading this or that book because it spoiled our appreciation or he thought it was incorrect. So by the end of the year we thought we knew everything there was to know! What a marvelous feeling, we were now in possession of the whole world and could relax! Of course the follow-

ing year Douglas Fraser came back and told us to read all the books
Wingert had cautioned against.

I came to life in graduate school. By a process of elimination I had
found a place that was not fraught with the dilemma of being Hungarian
and American at the same time. Although I started out with Africa, it
was not exactly Africa, but in some ways the whole globe that was this
magical place. Of course one could not belong and settle down in the
whole globe, it was purely a mental place, but at that point even a mental
place sufficed. These tribes had in common that they were traditional
cultures with some beautiful and some bizarre customs and they were
now either gone or in the process of disappearing in the face of
colonialism, missionary zeal and modernity. What we did in the courses
was to talk about them as they might have existed before white contact.
We were recreating a perfect and authentic past. Although I was
unconscious of it at the time, I now feel that for me they evidently stood
in for the Hungary of my childhood and my parents' world as yet undis-
turbed by outsiders. These reconstructed primitives were better than the
exile community in New York with its pathetically preserved culture
swamped by Americanism. Primitive cultures had the vitality I associated with Hungary's past in some ideal form. And yes, the primitives
were exotic in American thought just as I was perceived to be exotic.
From the day I set foot at the Cambridge School to the present I was and
still am seen as exotic. I carry it around like a scent. Had I studied Hungarian art, which some think I should have, I would have marginalized
myself totally and indeed might "never have had a job." But I had found
an exotic that was both accepted in the US and fitted my emotional
needs. I lost Hungary, but I gained the world. I could even say that this
field compensated for the loss of Hungary because I could have never
had it there. There is no "primitive" art history anywhere in Europe.

In America there was a lot of interest in Primitive Art in the late
1960's. Quite a number of students entered Columbia when I did wanting to study the same thing. Some of us became friends for life. My
closest friend was Cecelia Klein who became an Aztec scholar at UCLA.
George Preston is an Africanist studying Ghanaian kingdoms and who
has such a large collection that he created his own museum in Harlem.
George Corbin became an Oceania specialist at Lehmann College. The
four of us used to get into Preston's car and drive up to Riverdale to have

seminars with Wingert in his home with his collection. Although Wingert was in his seventies, he had a little toddler in diapers under foot of whom he was very proud. When Fraser came back, he had more official seminars with a dozen people and added Indonesia to our already colossal list of things and places to know. (Borneo masks, Sumbanese textiles, etc.)

Early on in my graduate school years Blaise and I went on a tourist trip to Mexico and traveled around. We saw most of the famous ruins, many of the museums, encountered natives sometimes dressed in regional costume and shopped for the delightful crafts available everywhere. I did fall in love with Mexico. It was a place more like the Hungary I remembered. The class structure with colorful if shabby peasants and overly decorated rich ladies, the folk arts, the chili peppers drying in the courtyards like paprika fitted into my ideas of a richly diverse culture. The mariachi bands reminded me of gypsy musicians. Nevertheless my interest was exclusively archaeological and the Indian past before the Conquest, generally referred to as "Pre-Columbian," i.e., before Columbus. I was not interested in the Colonial period with the snuffing out of Indian identity and the importation of European art.

Of all the ruins we saw I was most impressed by Teotihuacan – known locally just as "the Pyramids" because of its two huge constructions, one of which is as large as the biggest pyramid of Egypt. I looked on these two enormous constructions and the mile-long avenue near them and I felt overwhelmed by what these ancient people could do. Teotihuacan is dated about 1 A.D. to 700 A.D. and existed many centuries before the Aztecs. We do not know who built them, what language they spoke, what they thought. The name "Teotihuacan" comes from the Aztecs who called it "the place where the gods are made" in their own language. They apparently believed that it was built by the gods and not by humans. The Aztec buildings were smaller and less impressive. After the pyramids and the Avenue we visited the excavated habitations which were charming apartments with the rooms arranged around patios. I could imagine them filled with flowering cacti. Fragmentary mural paintings in bright colors were on some of the walls. I gathered that little had been written about them and I wanted to solve their mystery. There was one particular apartment, Tepantitla (also an Aztec name), that had some of the best murals with a personage emerging from the waves and presenting drops of water. Birds, flowers, and sea shells all around suggested life-giving rains and fertility.

This is what I wanted to work on, not knowing for many years later how it resembled the image of Szille in my childhood *Book of Lakes*. From my mental fascination with the "primitive" I found myself a real place in a Pre-Columbian home at Tepantitla. Of course, I still couldn't walk around in ancient Tepantitla, I could only be something of an archaeologist unearthing what it must have been like. Nevertheless, it was real, it had a floor and walls and murals and was not an intimidating structure like the pyramid but a place where people had lived and where in spirit I was to live for many years.

Teo (short for Teotihuacan) was not easy to study because we had no texts about it – the sixteenth century Spanish who wrote down so much got no information about it from the Aztecs. Most people thought that they must have been sort of like the Aztecs. I read everything that was written about it and described what I could in my dissertation but in no way did I manage to penetrate the mystery of this civilization. Wingert, who was the first to teach me about Pre-Columbian art too, did not like these ancient civilizations in the Americas. He thought their art was much too complicated and he preferred what he saw as the dramatic simplicity of tribal art. I was attracted to the complications and the mystery. I also saw ancient America as the Antiquity of the American continent – if Europe had Greece and Rome, the Americas had the Maya, Aztec and Inca. When I decided to become a "Pre-Columbianist" I somehow thought I was studying the earliest Americas, sort of starting my understanding of the New World at the beginning. It took me a while to see that people in the US don't consider these cultures as their origins but look to Europe and Greece and Rome after all. The subject of Indians, any Indians, might be a sore spot for a country that wrested their land away in a variety of ways. Some Latin American countries, especially Mexico, see the native heritage as their own, but generally the transplanted Europeans don't. Moreover, the surviving indigenous cultures are mostly too poor and too uneducated to claim, to understand, to study and to protect their heritage. So these great ruins of early civilizations in the Americas belong to no one and to everyone. I saw them as orphans, needing care, perhaps like myself, they had no parents who could take care of them physically or mentally. I was not modest: in Teo

I took the biggest, most impressive Pre-Columbian site under my wing – or perhaps it took me under *its* wing.

Nevertheless, I didn't get far with Teo; working on it was an experience of frustration and I decided to abandon it in favor of the Aztecs. The later Aztecs (1250-1519) had the advantage of being conquered by Cortez and a number of eyewitness accounts being written by him and his men who saw the capital city before it was destroyed. Missionaries wrote extensive accounts of politics, daily life, religion and even poetry. A great many intricately carved and polished sculptures survived the destructive zeal of the Spanish and were the glory of the beautiful Modern Museum of Anthropology in Mexico City. I thought that if I studied these texts and art works in detail, I might better understand what was special about Teo. In my research I found that there was no one place where I could find illustrations of all Aztec sculpture and I had to scramble from books to articles and make up my own corpus in xeroxes. It occurred to me that it would be practical to have a book that illustrated all, or nearly all, works of Aztec art. Since I was just starting out and had no experience writing books, this seemed like a small project. Martha Stewart's husband, Andy, was director of an art book publishing house, Harry N. Abrams, Inc., and I needed an art publisher for all the illustrations I wanted. That was a foot in the door and the project was accepted with the modification that I include all the arts: architecture, codices, featherwork, pottery, etc. the book then turned into a major undertaking but it was going to be the first book on Aztec art. It took seven years to write and research.

I made two major discoveries in the course of writing that book. The first one is that I found that each of the media did not represent the same subjects, or the same gods, and that there were obviously different cults and interest groups among the Aztecs, so we should not oversimplify it. Most significantly, I saw that the frightening death and sacrifice images were found on the monuments of the elite and seem to have been created for political reasons to scare their rebellious vassals into loyalty. The sculptures of ordinary people and temples were mostly benevolent and dealt with themes of fertility. There was no one Aztec art, there were many Aztec arts. I got to like the Aztecs. They were a complicated and interesting people. Their most amazing aspects are their engineering feats: causeways, aqueducts, artificial islands, canals, terracing and dikes show them to have been remarkably concerned with practical matters.

The second discovery in writing *Aztec Art* was that all those texts that I thought would be helpful in understanding Aztec are were not really helpful. In the end I sorted things out by type and appearance and archaeological context and trusted my eyes and reason. That made it possible to go back to Teo to see if sorting, looking, and archaeology would finally give the answers that eluded me before. Most importantly I could now see what was truly Aztec and how Teo differed. After years of work on the Aztecs I decided to return to Teo.

Aztec Art came out in 1983. The San Francisco de Young Museum received a bequest of over 70 Teo murals and fragments from an architect who had lived in the Bay Area. No one knew of Harald Wagner and his collection's existence until then. As Kathleen Berrin, the San Francisco museum curator, described him in the eventual publication, Harald Wagner was quite a character. An architect by training, he was also a painter and could take apart and put together diesel engines and musical instruments. He had a hacienda in Mexico. The murals were probably looted but were hard to sell. Who wanted to have a thick and crumbly wall fragment with irregular and flaking edges in their living room? Collectors want objects they can put on their mantelpiece or hang as if they were paintings. In the flea-market of Lagunilla I saw a number of faded Teo mural fragments with people bumping into them, getting smaller on every visit. You could not give away Teo murals. A few were in private collections, carefully mounted in heavy frames and sometimes significantly restored. But Wagner was not an ordinary man; he probably thought that he could put the murals back together like a puzzle and set up a beautiful green serpent in a cork-covered frame. He thought more like an architect with a wall than a collector with objects. He too tried his hand at restoration. However he came to the conclusion, that we came to later as well, that the murals could not be fitted together because too many intermediate pieces were missing. He tried to sell them to US museums, but no one wanted them and he left them to the de Young.

I was called in to help work on the murals along with Clara and Rene Millon. The Aztec field has many scholars: historians, historians of religion, economists, etc. The Teo field by contrast is very small. Perhaps only a dozen archaeologists specialize in it. During my work the most important were Rene Millon and George Cowgill who worked together on the most necessary project, a map of the city and of the valley of Teo. This map took many years and is the basis of most analyses. Until then the only structures known were the pyramids and the buildings along the Avenue. Millon's map, published as the *Urbanization of Teotihuacan*, demonstrated the apartment habitations all over the city and estimated a population near two hundred thousand. Rene's wife, Clara, was an expert on mural painting prior to my arrival on the scene. Among other things, George Cowgill was the computer expert dealing with an avalanche of data. He and Saburo Sugiyama are currently excavating the Pyramid of the Moon. Ruben Cabrera Castro has been directing many excavations along the Avenue. Linda Manzanilla has been exploring some of the many caves at the site. Although I cannot list everyone who has worked at Teotihuacan, these names indicate some of the most important persons and it's a relatively short list.

I had known the Millons since my dissertation and it was a pleasure to work with them on the new murals which put me back into a Teo project. This was the most hands-on work I have done with objects, trying to piece them together to figure out their sequence, literally moving them about and getting my hands dirty. They had been carved out of a muddy wall and were dangerously crumbly. The most exciting part of this project came in the summer of 1984 when Rene had an excavation at Teo to try to find where they had come from. The place was not only found – east of the Pyramid of the Moon – but new murals were discovered in the process. Because the area was not going to be restored, after being photographed and recorded the new murals were reburied. The area seems to have been very important and was one of the few places in which glyphs were found on the murals. Under Wagner's green serpent there was a row of flowering trees, each with a different glyph in its trunk. While we did not know what they meant exactly, they suggested the names of places and/or of plants. Until then Teo was known to have only a few glyphs in its art, which was strange in that the contemporary Maya and Zapotecs and the later Aztecs had highly developed writing systems. Teo was in contact with some of these cultures but did not adopt their writing system except very rarely. The question was why did Teo not have more written inscriptions since there evidently were a few. It was also striking that, as in the case of the Tepantitla mural, many of the paintings dealt with the benevolent aspects of nature, such as flowers and drops of water. The color green, which in Mexico is the color of the rainy season and of life, was very common in the murals. Evidently, most Teo paintings emphasized the goodness of nature rather than the horrific as in Aztec art.

Because the murals were likely to have been looted but belonged legally to the San Francisco de Young Museum, in a gesture of good will the museum chose to return a large number to Mexico. Tom Seligman who arranged this complex legal and political move put himself in a difficult position. The Mexican officials did not want to make too much of this return for fear of the press misinterpreting it and blowing it out of proportion. In the US he was criticized by many museum colleagues for giving back any of the murals because it set a precedent that could hurt them. All these stories were published in the 1988 book entitled *Feathered Serpents and Flowering Trees*.

As we were working on the murals, Tom Seligman and Kathleen Berrin had the idea of creating an exhibit of Teo art with me as guest curator. It was a wonderful project that went for all too many years, with untold number of trips to Europe and Mexico. There aren't that many Teo objects in collections, and we wanted all the important ones, for something we knew was not just a once in a lifetime occasion, but perhaps once in a century, perhaps not ever to be repeated. Teo objects were not valued as much as other Mesoamerican ones because they were not obviously aesthetic – they were not shiny, not realistic, not created with drama and/or an audience waiting to be wowed in mind. In other words, they were modest. There were no obvious deities. There were a lot of enigmatic masks in greenstone, alabaster, and basalt; there were strange incense burners with mask faces looking out through symbols, and even stranger there were figurines with a door in the chest that opened to reveal little figures on the inside. Much of Teo art was simplified and rectilinear. These objects would have to appeal to someone interested in modern and perhaps surrealist art from the West, not the general museum-goer. Why was Teo art so unusual in its own time? This was the assignment I gave myself and, in brief, I concluded for reasons we do not know, the Teo rulership kept a low profile with no images of themselves or inscriptions and the remaining imagery dealt mostly with nature. Because such a large number of people lived in apartment compounds in the city and were familiar with the persons, rituals, and ideas of their world, these were cryptically rendered for their own purposes and not dramatized and explained to people not in the know. I saw Teo as a great in-group.

Putting some of these ideas into the exhibition was difficult to begin with and then the San Francisco De Young Museum wanted Teo to look as gorgeous as other Pre-Columbian exhibitions did, and by dint of the marvelous objects we chose and fancy lighting it did indeed look spectacular. In those days exhibitions were advertised as "Treasures of..." or "Masterpieces of..." and "Teotihuacan: City of the Gods" was fitted into that mold. The catalogue, written by Mexican and US scholars, was an up-to-date synthesis of current knowledge. The exhibit did not travel, but in 1993 one hundred thousand people stood in line to see it in San Francisco and it was a great success.

I valued enormously the learning experience of searching for and exhibiting these objects and my many discussions with Kathleen Berrin who acquired a real feel for Teo. Now I felt that I finally had a story about Teo that eluded me in the dissertation and set about writing *Teotihuacan: An Experiment in Living* (1997). Except for Rene Millon's *Urbanization at Teotihuacan* and Eduardo Matos's *Teotihuacan: City of the Gods* (1990), there were hardly any books on Teo. I had to start in the beginning, which means that I argued that Teo was not like the Aztecs as everybody thought. I didn't fully know what Teo was like, but I thought I could reconstruct some kind of an identity for it. Most Mesoamerican cultures have a clear identity in our minds: for example we think of the Maya as aristocratic, elegant, artistic, intellectual. Teo lacked an identity and visibility which resulted in the fact that few studied it. Millions of people trek through the site of Teo and climb the Pyramid of the Sun every year having no clear idea of where they are and who made them. I wasn't sure that all my ideas were correct but I wanted Teo discussed.

I didn't subscribe to an old idea that Teo was "peaceful" since there were also plenty of representations of sacrifice and war. Hearts impaled on sacrificial knives on murals and vessels indicate that Teo sacrificed victims like all the rest of Mesoamericans. Moreover, recent excavations in the major pyramids have brought to light the skeletons of many sacrificial victims buried there. The difference was not between "warlike" or "peaceful" but more like between "aristocratic" and "egali-tarian," terms rarely used for ancient cultures in the Americas.

I was very impressed by the fact that most people at Teo lived in multiple apartment blocks rather than the thatched huts common in the rest of Mesoamerica. They must have had some power. There were about two thousand of them. These people also had access to those "modest" works of art such as incense burners and figurines. Many had access to mural painters – we don't know how many exactly because of the ruinous condition of the walls, but many in any case. By contrast the rulers and the elite did not make glorifying images of themselves proving their legitimacy also in writing. In fact, they shared some of the same "modest" objects. The impersonality of the most elaborate masks and figures of perhaps elite use were very different from the more per-sonal arts of other contemporary cultures. Besides, many Teo objects were mass-produced in molds for a large group of people.

Based on some of these facts it seemed to me that Teo had a corpo-rate society in which the rulers ruled with the help and consent of their citizens emphasizing their harmonious relationship rather than their conflict (all those beautiful scenes of verdant natures). There was some disagreement with other Teo scholars who emphasized the fact that such great pyramids could only have been built by very powerful rulers while I argued for the more communal structure of the city. In fact these two interpretations are not mutually exclusive – it is possible to have power-ful rulers and an organized community as I am learning in studying Inca Peru. But the Teo difference was the emphasis on organization and interaction rather than symbolic gestures by the rulers.

My other controversial suggestion for Teo was to see the figure in the Tepantitla mural as a female goddess. There is one colossal Teo sculpture that is clearly female and perhaps a goddess, and the goddess identity of the Tepantitla figure, though circumstantial, fits well with that. A major "female" deity fitted well with a society that did not seem to extol male power. I debated whether to present this figure as a "god-dess" or not, since arguments could be made either way. But I chose to go with the "goddess" idea because it brought out certain aspects of Teo and because I thought it would add human interest and material for debate. Some scholars are now questioning the goddess which is fine with me in that it shows that Teo issues are acquiring wider interest and discussion and that is precisely what I set out to do.

Teotihuacan is a part of me and always will be my Pre-Columbian home. However I gave what I could to it and it gave me a great deal in return, but it is time for me to move on. We may reconnect in the future. But at the moment I am pursuing some of the same issues with the Inca in South America. The Inca have been described as "benevolent" despots because all members of society were taken care of by the state. There were no beggars or paupers: everyone was put to work and received enough to live on. Some have described this as a wonderful, "primitive communism" while others see it as a soul-numbing totalitarianism. I am interested in finding out how this system worked, one way or the other. Unlike Teo that was frustrating because it had no textual sources, the Inca have many sixteenth century accounts to work from. Perhaps what I am after in the past is to find information on societies that were based less on conflict and more on mutuality and reciprocity. All positive models of social life my not be just in the democracy of Ancient Greece, but perhaps here in the reciprocal cultures of the Ancient Americas where we have not looked for them because we have been so preoccupied by sacrifice.

6
Things Fall Apart

"...the exile is someone who thinks imagination is a place."

Gustavo Perez Firmat

In 1973 I walked into a psychiatrist's office saying I had a perfect marriage, a loving husband, we had a lovely son, I had a Ph.D. and was teaching at Columbia University, and then I burst into tears. Blaise had been against my seeing a therapist – despite the fact that the famous early psychoanalyst Sándor Ferenczi had married into his family, he believed that psychoanalysts wreck marriages and should be avoided. But I was depressed with suicidal thoughts and needed help. Had I been in a "primitive" society I would have gone to a medicine man, witch doctor or shaman, but my modern option was the psychiatrist. I went and it was the first time I told my story.

All seemed to be well – Adam was born three weeks after I turned in my dissertation. We had a hard time finding him a name that would be the same in Hungarian and English. So I could go back to teaching, we hired Hungarian housekeepers whose English was nil, hoping that Adam would grow up learning Hungarian. In fact, Blaise and I spoke English together because we went to schools in America and our Hungarian was not sophisticated enough to express what he and I did all day. We moved into a large, old-fashioned apartment, ate the housekeeper's delicious Hungarian dinners, and began to live the way we imagined our parents did before the war. In that sense we fulfilled the immigrant dream and there was real joy in it. In time Blaise's elderly relatives died and my father came down with Parkinson's disease. His mother remarried and moved to Italy and mine went to Bethlehem. The older generation of "real" Hungarians was disappearing.

I didn't know what my malaise was, perhaps just an extended postpartum depression but I was lonely for company and started to think about Marc. Blaise worked long, hard hours as a young lawyer and was tired. We bought a house in Dingman's Ferry, Pennsylvania, not far from Lake Owassa. Dingman's was an edenic place in the woods with a pond, a rich wildlife of deer, wild turkey and bear and the charming village of Milford nearby. That too was a fulfillment since we now owned a piece of American land. There was room for my parents, for the housekeeper, and the rest of the family visited. Still, I was lonely and thought of Marc, who, according to a well- or ill-wisher, lived nearby on the Jersey side of the Delaware River. One day I took Adam by the hand and drove by to show him off and to satisfy my curiosity as to what happened to him.

He lived in a farmhouse that was once large and attractive but was now quite ramshackle. His wife, Mina, was an environmental activist fighting the Army Corps of Engineers who were planning to dam up the Delaware for electricity for Philadelphia and points south but would have left horrendous mudflats on the upper river. Our property was also threatened by this dam which luckily was never built. Marc was out there supposedly writing the great American novel – which everyone told him to do and which was more burden than reality. He was clearly unhappy with his life. Without discussing the subject it was apparent that our feelings towards each other had not changed since a decade ago. He said he'd return the visit sometime and I was sure he would, although in the end it took him more than a year to do so.

I was too restless to do scholarly research and perhaps too full of contradictory emotions so I took up writing fiction which I had last done at the Cambridge School of Weston. Except for one, the stories were fantasies and allegories. One however dealt with the dilemma of being both Hungarian and American which was ultimately related to my new-found desire to see Marc. Originally entitled "Return to Hungary" (1974) the story is about the first return visit of Hungarian exiles to communist Hungary. Stephen, a scholar interested in modern African literature, is there with his overbearing mother and his superficially silly American girlfriend. The crux of the story is that Stephen's mother wants Stephen to talk her nephew, Miklos, into emigrating to the West and is willing to finance it. Stephen finds this task distasteful but it actually leads to a serious discussion with Miklos which is the focus of his trip. Miklos is not interested in leaving, his family is full of tears and recriminations at the idea, and there is a farcical ending in which the girlfriend sheds Stephen for a more "authentic" Hungarian. Stephen is disgusted by both the Hungarians and Americans and takes off to Nigeria to interview Chinua Achebe, author of *Things Fall Apart* (1958), a book about a Nigerian traditional society that falls apart as a result of westernization. In the last line of my story Stephen asks Achebe: "What is it like to be a modern African writer, bridging the gap between the tribal past and the Western literary tradition?" In 1974 that was consciously emerging as my dilemma. I went to Africa or Latin America to escape the duality, and found it there too.

I was angry at my father for having cut my soul in half and not convinced that we had had to leave. I put these feelings into Miklos's words as he says "no" to leaving the country:

'Besides which, going away might not have solved the problem of indecision. I could still spend a lifetime wondering if I did the right thing to go. And that is what you returning tourists do. I don't mean you, because you did not make the decision, but your parents. They have a stake in proving that they made the right choice, they come back here to refuel their sense of rightness and to find new justifications for having left.'

'You stayed to have peace of mind?'

'Or at least to have the chance to think about something else. You don't know how liberated I felt by my decision to stay. Years of tension and preoccupation disappeared and there was a whole world of fascinating things I could do.'

What I had Miklos say was that he didn't want to live in emotional limbo all his life. He wanted it simple and he could have it simple. I could not; ambivalence was basic to my existence. I could never decide whether to call the story "Return to Hungary" or "Escape from Hungary," because it was both. The story was based on a real incident: my father trying to get my cousin Ambrus to leave Hungary for the West – anywhere. He refused and my father's brother Dezső was extremely angry that he wanted to take his one remaining child away. As Miklos indicates I (Stephen) had no choice in the matter since I was "brought." Tremendous anger began to well up in me at the fact that I was never asked whether I wanted to leave or not and was brought, so to speak, against my will. I asked myself was my father really in such danger or did he exaggerate?

How I yearned to be settled in one place like Miklos. I thought I had done that with Blaise and the Hungarian exiles. But "Little Budapest" in the East Eighties began to feel like a ghetto and not a real place. We were living in America but had very little to do with America except our jobs. There was something weird about it. Exile Hungarian attitude was that Americans, except for a few, are uncivilized and it's best to stay away from them. My feeling was that no matter how shallow or stupid Americans might be, I wanted to get to know them and live among them. There was no point in living in America if one did not live among Americans. I wanted to see for myself. Having been to the Cambridge School I thought I knew the good and bad side of Americans and I was not afraid of them. Besides Marc was my shining example of a smart American. Suppose I had made a mistake in 1963 and I should have stayed with Marc and assimilated into American life which had the virtue of being real?

Sometime later I went on a three month trip to Mexico and Guatemala exploring ruins slightly off the beaten tourist track. I took a boat down the Usumacinta to Seibal, quite overgrown with vegetation and authentic as all get out. I, who was still leery of flying, rented a small plane in Merida to see Yaxchilan and Bonampak, spent a week at Tikal marveling at the spider monkeys in the treetops, and found a car and driver to take me to the Honduras site of Copan driving over a dry riverbed. I was exploring the Maya contemporaries of Teo, feeling very much at home in the Pre-Columbian past. Chichicastenango in the highlands was especially wonderful with the Maya women dressed in the textile styles of their village. "One style – one village" was reminiscent of Wingert's classificatory approach. I couldn't resist buying a number of textiles and now they hang on my walls as beautiful pieces of modern art. Blaise joined me for a few days of more ruins and handicrafts and for the moment everything seemed to be fine.

In another five months or so Marc turned up as promised with the news that he would be in the city some of the fall. All was not well with his marriage. We did meet because it seemed fated, because we were young and stupid, and callous. Our spouses knew eventually and our happiness was surrounded by misery. We talked of a future together which was to be decided after the following summer.

When in doubt, seek the ruins. The summer of 1976 I spent with Adam exploring the ruins of the Southwest from Chaco Canyon to Pueblo Bonito. Adam was entertained by the cacti in botanical gardens and theme parks like that of the Flintstones. The days were ticking by slowly until I found out what lay in store for me.

Marc reappeared to say that he planned to stay with Mina and we parted. I cried a river of tears and then got on a plane to go to Paris for a conference where I had a nervous collapse. Fortunately nothing terrible happened, I got home all right but I was ill for months. Blaise was very good to me and probably hoped I learned a lesson and would no longer stray from "Little Budapest." I had learned nothing, however. I began to write *Aztec Art*, and in six months Marc was back since Mina left him for good. He was starting a new profession as a journalist living in the New Jersey farmhouse. I had learned something of a lesson and was not about to do anything foolish but seeing him on occasion proved irresistible. I think it was the childhood bond we shared. To make a long story short he eventually decided that for him the East Coast was hopeless and decided to move out to LA. He left as I was putting the finishing touches on *Aztec Art*. He wanted me to follow him to California. In 1983 the book was published, I got tenure at Columbia and moved to my own apartment on the West Side, alone and independent. Blaise argued that I could have as many lovers as I wanted to but it was my duty to fulfill the roles of wife and mother and stay. That was old-world Hungarian thinking and in my more mature wisdom I can understand it and even see it as reasonable. But I was in my thirties at the time and I thought this attitude was cruel and insulting and added fuel to the fire of marital distress. When I left Blaise I left the Hungarian community too since I was branded as a scarlet woman and felt shunned. All sympathy was on Blaise's side.

At the age of forty I tried to make myself an "American" life, but it wasn't easy. The Hungarian exiles may have been limited but they were a sheltering circle. There was no similar circle among the Americans I knew. Perhaps it was something European. My parents had a circle of interesting people consisting of doctors, lawyers, and artists. I have my professional friends but they are all over the US. Various people recommended that I join a church. So even though I don't believe in Christian dogma I had nothing to lose and tried going to church. For a while I tried

Riverside Church, the Cathedral of St. John the Divine and even a funky Unitarian church that had neo-pagan, Wiccan rituals. It was all an interesting experience but I did not "click" with anyone through church. I did learn that there were a lot of lonely people and if things were really bad churches can come to your aid.

I agreed to spend three months in Malibu with Marc to see if I would consider joining him in California. It was clear from the beginning that I could not make the leap from New York to Los Angeles, that the move from Budapest to New York was about as far as I could go. Besides, Adam was twelve and I could not leave him. (Adam now lives in California.) But while I was there, Marc showed me California with the knowledge and zest of a reporter, from Pasadena to San Francisco, that I value enormously. The flowers were blooming in a riot, the Pacific was lapping at the shore, the climate was heavenly. The Greene and Greene houses were fascinating. And everywhere there was a hybrid vigor from Mexican-Korean to Japanese-Chicano neighborhoods and restaurants. "Authenticity" had no meaning in Los Angeles and that made it feel fresh and young. Marc and I remained friends – we are each other's oldest friends – but we parted finally.

I was left completely alone, still hoping to find some partner and life situation that would be suitably "American." I had become reasonably independent which was certainly an American virtue. Thanks to Columbia I had a spacious apartment overlooking the Hudson River that is as splendid as my childhood home in Budapest. Though divorce made me poorer, some luxuries came my way. Once I was asked to lecture on a four-masted schooner, the Sea Cloud, that was made for Marjorie Merriwether Post. There were about as many workers on the ship as the sixty exclusive guests and I had my own stateroom. For all that, I only had to give one lecture on the Maya and mingle with the guests. The guests were an impressive group of doctors, lawyers, and even an opera singer. Having gone with Adam on an Alaska cruise to see glaciers the year before, I learned that on a cruise you need a different outfit every night. I came prepared even with an exotic Maya garment I had bought in Chichicastenango.

Wayne accosted me with surprisingly specialist questions indicating that he had read up on the Maya. He turned out to be a brilliant mathematician of varied interests and some significant means, scuba-diving his way through the Caribbean. He was a Southerner with a base in Chicago. Afterwards we saw each other regularly but at long intervals, dining in good places and going to the symphony. We went on trips to Florida, the Grand Canyon, Las Vegas, and he guided me through the symbol of the South, Charleston. I got to know Chicago a bit and wondered what it would be like to live there. It was somewhat disquieting that he seemed to have no friends in Chicago and that his friends were all over the world. He was a loner and he seemed to want to stay that way. The relationship was not going anywhere near a settled form. Eventually my attention was diverted by post-communist Hungary and its exciting new developments. We spent a short time in Hungary when I had my apartment – which he considered too small – but Hungary was not Wayne's place of fantasy. He was more interested in Russia. Like most Americans he didn't like the nationalism of Hungarians which comes with the territory. One year he took me to Romania, for which I am grateful since I would have never gone alone. I got to see my mother's home town, Marosvásárhely. He seemed to like Romania with Count Vlad's ("Dracula's") castle better. It was very sad to lose this relationship because I so hoped that Wayne would be the American husband I was looking for. Perhaps I was too exotic for him because he later married a college sweetheart.

I saw a great deal of America, but I was singularly unsuccessful in settling in an American spot when the real Hungary reemerged as a possibility and I moved in that direction with many of my fellow exiles like lemmings over a cliff. I began to notice my pendulum swings from America to Hungary and back and history repeating itself and wondered what on earth I was doing. As I was interested in Latin American literature I once picked up a book by Gustvao Perez Firmat, *Life on the Hyphen*, which explained my strangely aberrant behavior for the first time.

Perez Firmat was a Cuban refugee who came to the US after Castro's revolution as a teenager – he was eleven. He lived in Miami in the Cuban district known as "Little Havana" but has now become mainstream. As he tells it, his life has been a long, tortuous identity crisis in which his loyalties were torn between Cuba and America and he always felt that he had to make a choice between them. Perez Firmat's book is about being an involuntary immigrant – brought as a teen during a political crisis – and the problem assimilation poses when it is against one's will. He described this kind of person as a 1.5 generation exile. The first generation person, as he describes it, one who came to the US after eighteen, remains forever foreign in psychological make up even if he or she lives in the US all their life. The second generation, the children who came over very young or who were born here of the original immigrants, are American despite their parents' best efforts to inculcate foreign ways into them. But the 1.5 generation persons who came here in their crucial teen years tend to feel that they belong equally strongly to both their cultures which results in a great deal of internal turmoil. Their life is a constant balancing act between two mutually contradictory cultural imperatives that makes them guilty of betrayal whichever way they turn.

Perez Firmat did not invent the idea of the 1.5 generation person. A Cuban-American sociologist, Ruben Rumbaut, first defined it in the study of Indochinese children in 1991: "...members of the '1.5' generation form a distinctive cohort in that in many ways they are marginal to both the old and the new worlds, and are fully part of neither of them." ("The Agony of Exile: A Study in the Migration and Adaptation of Indochinese Refugee Adults and Children.") The idea is no older than the 1990's. Moving back and forth between Blaise and Marc, America and Hungary, I seemed to be a textbook case. Perez Firmat saw three stages in the life of the exile: "substitution" in which the person tries to find some equivalent of the old country and lives in the imagination as if that were a real place, followed by "destitution" – the realization that this is impossible and one is not living in the real world at all. When "things fell apart" for me I was entering a long phase of "destitution." Perez Firmat's advice to overcome these is assimilation, which he named "institution." The way to do this was to marry American. Now I had been trying to marry American unsuccessfully and perhaps I wasn't fully ready for it because it did not happen.

Perez Firmat's major concern is what will happen when Castro dies and Cuba becomes free – what will the exiles do, go back or stay? He suggests that some will return. "Once the 'real' Cubans go back to the island, those of us who remain here will have no choice but to realize that we are Americans." This anxiety about the availability of Cuba prompts another observation: "Paradoxically, for someone like myself, returning to Cuba would be tantamount to going into exile the second time."

It was possible to go back to Hungary after 1989, and though I did not go back permanently, I spent the better part of a decade involved with Hungary and Hungarian matters. It helped my 1.5 generation self in that I got to know the real Hungary as opposed to the nostalgic version and I gained a lot of valuable information sometimes painfully acquired. I had a wonderful time doing it and it gave me a clearer sense of who I was and where I came from. But it postponed my possible settling or assimilation in America.

7
The Real Hungary

"He is not a genius...whose longing for his homeland
stopped him from knowledge of the big world...."
Tivadar Csontváry

In 1989 the wall came down in Berlin and all the Eastern European countries held hostage by the Russians were free. There were free elections and not surprisingly a conservative party backed by many exiles came into power in Hungary. Since then they were highly contested by a newly formed Socialist party that was in some ways a continuation of the communist leadership. While for some years there was a euphoria of rejoining the West and the prosperity to come, in time there was some nostalgia for the benefits of the communist era. To be sure not for the killings and torture but for the entitlements of generous pensions, national health care and even free vacations in worker resorts. Artists had resorts as well. While these were modest by Western middle-class standards, they were by lakes and woods with good country cooking and offered by the state for free. No matter how much the opposition explains that these benefits bankrupted the state and could no longer be sustained, many have since voted to return the socialists to power in the hopes of reviving a social safety net they came to value. While the older generation is still struggling with nostalgia, the younger generation has learned entrepreneurship and many entered the ranks of new million-aires, accentuating the differences between the haves and the have-nots that is distressing Hungarian society.

All of this was not yet clear when I became a frequent visitor to Hungary. Actually I had been to Hungary a couple of times in the 1970's when the dictator János Kádár officially "forgave" all those Hungarians who left the country and allowed us back to visit and spend hard currency much needed by the country. Those occasions with Blaise and once with Adam and my nephew Gregory were nostalgic and fun. We visited my old home on Otto Herman Street where nothing had changed, my old school, the old Catholic church and supermarket; we went to Baja to see my Uncle Feri and his second wife Ilonka in Owl Castle, my friend Edda Kubinyi and her son Miki who was Adam's age and several hundred of Blaise's relatives. We ate a lot of wonderful Hungarian cooking both with friends and in restaurants cheap for American dollars. The restaurants catering to tourists played schmaltzy gypsy music but we could escape to the opera and listen to first-class classical music for pennies. Nothing much seemed to be for sale in the shops and we brought substantial gifts and bags of clothes to friends and relatives. It was on one of those occasions that Uncle Feri presented me with two books, which turned out to be my and my sister's favorite. *The Book of Lakes* was mine. Feri recounted how after hearing of our escape in 1956 he immediately went up to Budapest with a truck and loaded it full of our furniture, rugs, china, whatever he deemed important or portable and took it down to Owl Castle in Baja. We also found out from the superintendent that a neighbor had adopted our cat and she had a good home. I guess whatever else was left was taken by people in the building. My mother could not bear to hear stories of this final dispersal of our things; perhaps she preferred to think of it as we had left it. Besides, Uncle Feri had written some very nasty letters about "how could you leave your country, you traitors…" which she never forgave. Someone, probably a communist, was moved into our old apartment. That person was away on one of my visits and the super let me in so I could see the apartment – I wanted to verify that it was as large as I remembered it. It was, still spectacular even by American standards with the windows and the mountain view.

The nostalgia part of the return to Hungary I did several times and was not interested in pursuing any more. I had done it. I was no longer interested in my parents' Hungary, the in times the nineteen-thirties, forties, and even my childhood in the fifties. I became interested in what Hungary was in the present, in the nineteen-nineties in my own time as an adult. My interest was stimulated by the arrival of a remote cousin, Emese Boda, and her boyfriend, Zsolt Farkas, to New York. In the their late twenties, they came to work and to make enough money to buy an apartment in Budapest. (Budapest has almost no rental market, only ownership.) They talked me into painting my apartment which was accompanied by a great deal of conversation in Hungarian since their

English was very limited. They found my Hungarian hilariously funny! Now I had worked hard to maintain my Hungarian, spoke quite fluently, could read and write. And that was the trouble since I had maintained a nineteen-fifties Hungarian and the language had moved on. They broke up over my "archaic" expressions and while I enjoyed their new expressions I found it strange to say them myself. I was a living fossil. As I saw in Hungary, the language had also acquired a different tonality, more of a sing-song than what I was used to. When I went to the hairdresser in Budapest as soon as I opened my mouth the woman asked "Where is the lady from?" I could not pass as a Hungarian because I had an American accent. These were shocks. Here I was thinking I was a "genuine" Hungarian and I wasn't. I wasn't a "genuine" American and I was not a "genuine" Hungarian. What was I exactly?

Emese and Zsolt were quoting to me a poet, by the name of Pilinszky, that I had never heard of and insisted that he was the greatest Hungarian poet of all time. I was surprised. They mentioned a painter, Csontváry, who was also considered to be the greatest Hungarian painter of all time and whose name was totally unfamiliar. Besides my linguistic backwardness I was evidently also culturally backward. Things had changed in the years that I had been gone, Hungarian culture was not the same. If I wanted to belong I had serious remedial studying to do. I was eager to learn about Pilinszky and Csontváry as much as about the way people live from hairdressers up and down. One way to do it was through my profession.

As Hungary opened up I was interested in getting to know the anthropologists working on American Indian subjects and presented myself as a fellow specialist. Art History in Hungary and in Europe does not include Pre-Columbian, it is all under anthropology. Budapest has a very fine Ethnographic Museum and an Anthropology Department at the University. I brought a selection of my books and it was suggested by my Hungarian colleagues that I take off a semester and teach in Budapest. They were experts in the mechanism of how to do this. They said to apply for a Fulbright grant to teach and once I got the grant I would be selected by them automatically. This was a very exciting possibility – spending a semester in Hungary, retooling the language and lecturing at the University of Budapest in Hungarian! Returning to my home country as a specialist in Ancient America and sharing what I had learned in the

years abroad. Getting to know the scholars and others in Budapest in the
here and now, and moving into Budapest life. I imagined how happy my
mother would be, although in fact she was not happy. She would have
been happier if I had been lecturing in Paris.

In Hungary I spent much time visiting with Edda whose friendship
had been lifelong. We were the same size and exchanged clothes. She
enjoyed going to places and we visited towns like Sopron and Eger. In
Eger I was curious to see the remains of the castle in the story with the
Turks, but of course not much remains. There is a lot of wonderful regional baroque style in Hungary and we both enjoyed the traditional. She
is a music lover and we went to the opera many times, where she knew
all the singers by name and reputation. Budapest is a small place and
people know each other and that appealed to me. We went to the pool at
the Hotel Gellért because that was my favorite since going to pools with
my mother as a girl. Budapest has a lot of natural springs and spas. The
Gellért pool was too expensive for locals and was frequented mainly by
German tourists but I liked it anyway. Edda often invited me to their
house by Lake Balaton and we spend many lazy days idly chatting on
the grassy beach between swims. One could live well in Hungary with
American money. Newfound friends included Kati Klimes who worked
at the University Library and who met me by offering to translate *Aztec
Art* into Hungarian. Nothing came of that or of other translation and
publication attempts since my material was judged too "esoteric" and too
expensive to produce. Anyone seriously interested can read it in English.
I can thank János Gyarmati of the Ethnographic Museum who repub-
lished an article and interview in their journal *Tabula* and that is as far as
I've gotten in print in Hungarian. János had done excavations in Mexico
and Bolivia and one could discuss Aztecs, Incas, and Teo with him. I
enjoyed my friendship with Eva Körner, which started in New York
when she rented my apartment for a month. Eva's field is twentieth
century art in Hungary and she has been called the "goddess of modernism" by some who didn't like her influence. She knew everyone in the
Hungarian art world. With some of these friends I went to local art
exhibits and trips to Szentendre, a picturesque artists' colony, a short
train ride away. One of the highlights there for me is the Ferenczy
Museum which has the bronze sculpture of my twelve year old head. Its
an amazing feeling to be there in three dimensions. (Béni also made a

terracotta bust of me that may be in a private collection – I have never seen it.) Some years Szentendre had marvelous ice creams and restaurants with plenty of venison and wild boar on the menu. Wild boar paprika is sensational.

One day sitting in the grass by Lake Balaton I felt depressed and Edda tried to cheer me up. Wayne was being remote. Blaise had remarried a younger woman who was more Hungarian than I was, and presumably less trouble, and he had bought a house in a fashionable district of Buda. He convinced his firm to open a legal office in Budapest. He had practically moved back to Hungary. Some years after our divorce we became friends, or more properly "relatives." We found that because of our similarity there were certain things we alone could understand and appreciate and sometimes turned to each other for support. Before his marriage, there was brief talk between us of reconciliation and we mentioned the possibility of a house in Budapest. This was at the time of the euphoria of Hungary becoming free. But nothing had come of that either. I had just been telling Edda of the apartment Emese and Zsolt had bought for a remarkably small sum in dollars and that perhaps I could buy myself such a small apartment. Edda was trying to talk me into looking for a place, with the motto that there is no harm in looking. It seemed pointless since I was leaving soon but she insisted on coming over the next day and looking at real estate.

She arrived with various newspaper ads by owners and proceeded to call the numbers. Most were not at home or had answering machines. I said I wanted an apartment in Pest, downtown. Although I had grown up on the more elegant Buda side of the Danube with its trees and gardens, as a single person I didn't want to sit in the grass, I wanted to be near the museums, the opera and theatres, the whole downtown shopping world at Pest. Pest is flat and built up with houses and full of activity. Moreover, as a child I never got to know Pest which was a "grown up" place. One number answered and we went over to have a look. It was a building built before 1920 with high ceilings and charming moldings. There was one all-purpose room and an eat-in kitchen. The only thing wrong with it was that it was at the end of a courtyard and dark. However, it was near the Hotel Astoria, a Budapest landmark, and two long blocks away from the shopping and tourist streets. One could not have been any more central. But it was much too dark. As we were talking with the owners they said they must sell because they were emigrating to New Zealand. Would they sell the furniture? Yes. Would they sell the knives and forks in the drawer? Would they sell the complete contents of the apartment? Yes. I calculated for a few minutes the convenience of having a fully furnished apartment the next time I came to teach instead of running around looking for lights and wastebaskets. The darkness didn't seem too bad since I would not be living there full time. What were my chances of finding another deal like this in the short time I was there? We came to an agreement, went to see Blaise's law partner who prepared the papers and by the time I went to bed I was the owner of an apartment in Budapest, the most extravagant impulse buying I have ever done. I was up all night with nerves and pains and panic. As it turned out, I had made a wonderful decision. Emese and Zsolt repainted the place and I had a home in Budapest waiting for me to come home to.

However, I had counted my chickens before they hatched. I received the Fulbright grant all in good time, took off the semester from Columbia, planned my teaching in Budapest and told everyone I was leaving. Then I was informed that the Hungarian Fulbright Committee changed its mind and no longer wanted me to come and teach. I absolutely could not believe it. How could they do such a thing to me as I was so eager to bring my talents to Hungary? I never found out completely what happened since various committees and persons blamed each other and assured me of their dismay. There were a number of possibilities: that someone else appeared whom they wanted more, or that they wanted more of an American and less a Hungarian-American, or that I was a threat to a particular person who wanted to remain the foremost American Indian specialist in Hungary. All of these could have been the reason. The fact remains that they invited me and then they rejected me. That taught me a lesson not to trust my homeland which generally didn't like expatriates unless, like George Soros, they came with a lot of money. Any idea I may have had about going back to Hungary and blending in either temporarily or permanently was nipped in the bud. In the US I was in an awkward situation not wanting to admit that I was rejected by my own country and having made the preparations to go, having bought an apartment, I decided to go anyway and work on my own projects. Not having to teach a course in Hungarian was in some ways a relief. I didn't need to teach more, I needed to write more. I could relax and eventually I did.

January 1994 I packed excitedly for a six-month stay in Budapest, taking winter and summer things with me and what I wanted in the apartment. It looked like I was moving. Surprisingly, my American friends disapproved of what I was doing and were annoyed with me. I was being an ingrate having been given refuge in America in wanting to go back to my homeland. The American myth is that the refugee arrives, thanks God to be the in US and never looks back except in some small symbolic way. Not five suitcases and an apartment. It was difficult to leave with angry friends in the doorway. I seemed to be displeasing both Hungarians and Americans by this move. In Hungary I learned quickly not to say I was from the US or how long I was there for. I was often asked if I had come back to retire, of course, as an American millionaire and there was a great deal of envy in the question. At other times there was a concern that I was moving back taking a job away from a Hungarian. I also learned not to mention that I left in 1956 because that was interpreted that I was a traitor and an opportunist. I learned to say that I was a Canadian who left as a small child knowing nothing from nothing. I now know that expatriates are disliked everywhere. They didn't share the good and bad times with their compatriots, they don't know what's going on, their allegiance is not clear. (I knew from the beginning that expatriates were not likely to get far in the Middle East.) It wasn't just the Fulbright Committee, pedicurists and taxi drivers alike mistrusted expatriates. Americans mistrust those who won't assimilate and hold on too long or too tightly to their places of origin. No one wants a person who is half this and half that. (As the Hungarian saying goes, "You can't ride two horses with one butt.")

Nevertheless I wanted to experience Hungary whatever I might learn in the process and despite annoyed goodbyes and a lack of welcome, I went. I bought the apartment in such a hurry I didn't really know where it was. I didn't know Pest and had only a vague idea of the location of the Hotel Astoria and the Jewish Synagogue it was near. The first thing I did was to make a large scale map of my own neighborhood so I'd know the nearby streets. Budapest felt like home but was as foreign as any other unknown city.

I visited Uncle Feri with his second wife Ilonka in Baja and saw with great concern that a great many things had been stolen recently. I remembered his paintings of what I had called "squinty eyed" saints in the living room done in the 1930's but they were mostly gone. Feri, who was ninety, blamed it on the local gypsies but with the stubbornness of an old man would not change the locks and didn't seem to care. He did not seem to want to change anything. In about a month he died and I was down for the funeral. Drying her tears Ilonka advised me that now that he was dead and I had an apartment in Budapest I could take my parents' belongings and furniture. It seemed best to do this soon before the gypsies emptied the whole house. I gave the cheap furnishings in my apartment to Edda's son Miki and hired a truck to bring the things to Budapest. There were two thirties-ethnic rugs designed by my father and Feri, my father's desk, supposedly a Renaissance table, a couple of Biedermayer chairs, the round table that was in our children's room in Buda, a Venetian mirror and a variety of smaller pieces. All of a sudden my apartment was transformed into my childhood home and it gave me a tremendous feeling of satisfaction. Irmuska, my charming elderly neighbor, advised me on how to get the rugs clean and had a nephew who did upholstery. I was busy putting things to rights. I was grateful and visited Ilonka several times in Baja to be there for her in her bereavement. I had a life in Hungary.

My Budapest days were like my New York days when I am not teaching. I worked on my projects, I went shopping for food and necessities in the local stores like my neighbors, I popped into the local boutiques to see if there were new clothes (usually German manufactures), I bought a pastry or two, I checked out the bookstore in my building, I got the mail. Greater expeditions were to museums, antiquarian shops, hairdressers, and visits. On Sundays Edda often made traditional family lunch, asking what were my favorites. I tried reciprocating but cooking was more cumbersome than in the US and we went to restaurants. Zsolt came occasionally for a long philosophical discussion and smoked up the house. Blaise and I sometimes went to the Gellért for a swim and if the weather was good we had lunch in the restaurant on the terrace. An investment in a little espresso maker was essential in that all Hungarians drank strong espresso. After that first long visit I went back to my Budapest apartment for two or three months every summer when my teaching at Columbia was over and followed pretty much the same routine for years. Half my life was in the US, but the exciting half was in Hungary.

In Budapest I was an anthropologist. I listened to everyone's political opinions without taking sides. I listened to life histories. I tried to figure out what my life would have been like had I stayed. I came to the conclusion that my generation was sort of a lost generation with a very limited but not uncomfortable life. Hungary was freed in their fifties which was too late for them because they were close to retirement and could not easily retool their life. At best, I could have been a respected professional who traveled abroad like my cousin Ambrus. There is no question that my opportunities were much greater having gone to the US. But then Hungarians had a certain satisfaction in having survived those bad times and having come out all right. In many ways they had more peace of mind than I did. They were rooted and I was a floater.

One of my great joys was the Hungarian language. It usually took me a month to get into the local lingo and pass for a native. As I was trying to define what "hungarianness" was, it became clear that it was the language. There is a general belief that Hungarian is the most difficult language in the world. This is not completely true. There is a large community of Chinese in Budapest who speak excellent Hungarian as do many students from all over the world in the local universities. The American writer Edmund Wilson learned Hungarian and was flattered that his plays were translated. He even wrote Hungarian quite well. People learn difficult languages when necessary – but most people are reluctant to learn an obscure language spoken by only fifteen million people of no practical use to them. Which means that Hungarian is the precious possession of that fifteen million who believe that it is the most "musical," "elegantly economical," "rational" and "aesthetic." It is so, in fact, because it is a work of art that has been created over time.

Until about 1800 Hungarian was a vernacular spoken by the lower classes. The official language of the Austro-Hungarian empire was Latin. (As the quip puts it: A well-born man of the world speaks German to his dog, English to his horse, Hungarian to his coachman, French to his mistress and Spanish to his God.") In 1784 Joseph II declared that German would be the language of the empire and the Hungarians began to brush off their language for official use as a sign of nationhood.

Starting at the end of the eighteenth century a group of language reformers tinkered with the various dialects for nearly a century making up new grammatical constructions, endings, thousands of new words creating the present "rational and beautiful" language. This goes on today as expressions are found for all the technical and computer technology coming out of English. Of course the language of the sciences is English. One thing we Hungarians like is that unlike English, Hungarian is totally phonetic. Hungarian is often amusing and especially so in the variety of cursing. Unlike the repeated "f-word" in English, Hungarian countrymen can curse for an hour without using the same expression twice, much to the enjoyment of their hearers. I was listening to individuals speak with their own idiosyncratic expressions, the current slang, the official newspeak, all in a living, changing entity different from our limited exile hemming and hawing.

People ask me, should they learn Hungarian, what should they read? Who is the great novelist? Alas Hungary has no one world class novelist, the great writers are mostly poets. In my day Endre Ady, the symbolist poet living in Paris, was considered the greatest but since major publications in 1957 János Pilinszky has received that honor. It is characteristic that we exile provincials did not hear about him. Like Aztec poetry, Hungarian poetry is philosophical about issues of life, death and love. As soon as I read Pilinszky in my catching up, I wanted to translate his poems into English. I was less concerned with meter and rhyme and more with the straight sense of the words to reflect the unpretentiousness and terseness of the language. I could only handle short poems but they were packed with intensity and passion.

> *October 14, 1970*
> *I cried. Afterwards my back was moist,*
> *My clothes wrinkled, my hand asleep.*
> *I desired to cover my limbs*
> *So what you embrace should be*
> *What every genuine embrace seeks:*
> *The surrender of a wild animal.*

Few people read poetry in any case and great deal is lost in any translation so that a country whose primary literature is poetry is out of luck on the world stage. It makes Hungarian culture that much more of a secret society in which you are lucky if you happen to have been initiated but you can't share.

The other "great" who I did not know existed and had to find out about was the painter Tivadar Csontváry Kosztka (pronounced "Chontvare"). There was now a museum devoted to his works in Pécs. I was amazed by the size of the paintings, the bold color, the non-Hungarian subjects, and the idiosyncratic style. Csontváry was cosmopolitan and naïve at the same time. Scholars debate whether he was mad and to what extent. A great painting like the cedar of Lebanon with people dancing around it taps into anyone's unconscious. The Csontváry story is as good as the paintings.

Its an accidental miracle that Csontváry's paintings were saved at all. He died as an unsuccessful, old, and insane artist in 1919 in Budapest. A young architect, Gedeon Gerlőczy, was going by the house with his friends and saw a "for rent" sign and went in to inquire. He heard the relatives discussing a major auction to be held the next day when the big, worthless paintings would be sold to truckers as tarps. He saw them gather up papers. The studio was already rented and he went off to have drinks with his friends. Gerlőczy couldn't get what he had seen out of his mind and went back that night to acquire the papers and he turned all he had into cash so that the next day he could bid for the entire contents of the studio and bought it. The truckers who were counting on the canvases were in such a fury that only through physical violence did Gerlőczy get away from them. This collection is in the Pécs museum since 1973.

In Hungary, Csontváry only became known and popular in the late sixties and seventies. I have books on Twentieth Century Hungarian art that have only a brief mention of him. Although he had an exhibit in Paris in 1949 which was appreciated by Picasso who recommended it to Chagall, he had no critical success. Despite modern accolade, Csontváry is still not known or exhibited much outside Hungary; he hasn't hit a nerve.

Csontváry was a pharmacist and the idea of painting came to him in 1888 when he was twenty-seven years old. An internal voice told him that he would be the world's greatest plein air painter, greater than Raphael! He accumulated money so he could be trained in Germany and France and sold his pharmacy. In 1902 he embarked on a great journey through the Balkans, Greece, and on to Egypt and Jerusalem. He carried with him some enormous canvases – Baalbek is almost 4 x 7 meters, and even his small canvases are close to a meter in width. His artistic activity lasted about ten years and he had over one hundred paintings. Insanity cut short his activity.

I was first impressed by all the ruins in the Csontváry paintings which reminded me of Ancient America. The Greek "Theater at Taormina" (1904) with its cheerful color, the arches glowing red against a yellow sky against the large expansive of bright blue water. When I show Americans pictures of Csontváry's paintings they usually ask, perplexed, "yes, but where are the landscapes of Hungary?" It seems to be axiomatic that a "regional" painter should paint his region. Santa Fe artists are expected to paint the deserts of New Mexico, Maine artists paint the islands of Maine. Many Hungarian artists do paint Hungarian scenes. But Csontváry was going to become a great "Hungarian" painter by leaving Hungary. It is clear from his writings that Csontváry was going East, retracing the footsteps of the original Hungarians in mythology. In Csontváry's day the Hungarians were associated with the Scythians, the Huns and the Near East. In painting Taormina, Baalbek and Jerusalem, he was painting Hungarian and Western ancestry in a larger sense. Baalbek has graceful cedars near the columns, but the focus is on a large stone "sacrificial altar" which was associated with Attila the Hun in Csontváry's writings. Nevertheless, in the paintings there is no Attila, no Hungarians, no one except tiny locals and camels. The paintings are cosmic in the grandeur of nature and man's activity in it. Csontváry is perhaps the only Hungarian painter whose works are not local but universal, despite his interest in Hungarian origins.

Unfortunately, the voluminous surviving writings prove that Csontváry was a crank who turned out pedantic booklets with titles like "The Cultured Man's Mistake," "The Genius: Who can be and Who can't be a Genius." "He is not a genius…who has been shaken in faith and stopped in the middle of the road,…whose longing for his homeland stops him from the knowledge of the world, who drinks alcoholic beverages..." – a rant for pages and pages. I fell for Csontváry and his obsession. He may have been mentally ill but he has to have been reasonably sane to do his trip and paint the great canvases he did.

It is impossible to deal with Hungarians without the issue of their origins coming up. Hungarians speak a non-Indo-European language in the midst of Indo-European speakers. How did that come to be? According to histories written in the Middle Ages, they came from somewhere in the East and settled around 900 A.D. in the Carpathian basin. They were led by their chief, Árpád, shown in paintings on a white horse, and they went raiding through Europe as far as Paris. Europeans thought they were like the Huns, a similar horse-riding nomadic people who wreaked havoc four hundred years earlier and their names – Hungarians, Hongrois – come from the Hun. Actually the Hungarians called themselves and their language "Magyar" but were happy to be associated with the Huns and their leader Attila. Attila is a common Hungarian name. "Attila, The Sword of God" was a popular rock opera in the 1980's. As early as the thirteenth century Hungarians such as Brother Julianus set out to find their ancestors in Asia. In the early nineteenth century Sándor Körösi Csoma started out in Transylvania and went on foot across Baghdad and Teheran all the way to Tibet. He didn't find the mythical homeland but he became the first Tibetan scholar. Another world traveler, András Jelky, had a statue in Baja where he was born in 1783. He started out as a conscript and slave who visited as far as Jakarta and ended up the Dutch ambassador to Japan. The search for the Asiatic origins of Hungarians has been going on for centuries without proof positive. Anthropologists think that Hungarian may be related to some Siberian languages such as Vogul. I have read that we are related to the Native Americans who came across the Bering Straits while some audacious scholars relate Hungarians to the Maori of New Zealand and the ancient Sumerians of Mesopotamia.

Most recently, however, the search for exotic origins has ceased and the popular theory is that only a very few actually migrated from wherever in the East and the vast majority of the population is European and has been there since Paleolithic times speaking Hungarian. It is hard to avoid the impression that politics plays a part in these origin scenarios. The Asiatic image of the Hungarian was perhaps created and fostered in the nineteenth century to counter Western Austrian hegemony. The idea that we have always been Western seems related to the current pro-Western desire to be part of Europe where it is now said we have always been. This pro-Westerness is supported by the subsequent history of chief Árpád whose royal descendant, Stephen, accepted Western Christianity which he preferred to Eastern Orthodoxy in 1000 A.D. King Stephen became a saint. St. Stephen is honored as much in Hungarian history as Árpád. The same man who created the rock opera "Attila" created a rock opera about St. Stephen. DNA may or may not solve the issue of the ethnic racial origins of the Hungarians especially since there have been admixtures with Germans, Slavs, and Turks over the years. In any case, Hungarians have created for themselves a dual persona – partly Asiatic, partly Western. What I found striking is how many scholars, amateurs and travelers have spent time, energy and money on trying to pin down the racial and ethnic identity of Hungarians. We are a culture still trying to figure out where we belong. More likely, as has been suggested by Tamas Hófer, the former head of the Ethnographic Museum, Hungarians prefer to remain borderline between East and West so they can lean in one direction or the other as circumstances demand. Now I know why I have no trouble seeing myself as both Western and Non-western.

Hungarians have always traveled, not necessarily just looking for their origins. It's a small country, one has to get out to see the world. I haven't been anywhere that a Hungarian had not already been to. (My work as a Pre-Columbian art historian has been preceded by Pal Kelemen in the 1940's, and the first person with a camera in Mexico was the Hungarian Pál Rosti in the nineteenth century.) At a secondhand bookstore in Budapest I bought a book entitled *Hungarian Wanderers of Five Continents* published in 1937 which chronicled the story of sixteen individuals. But the reason I really bought it is that the previous owner had penciled in forty other names not in the book. I knew many he didn't know either. Hungarians keep track of who went where and accomplished what and periodically collect them in a book such as *Hungarian Researches of Faraway People* (1978). I found myself a slot in very good company: I am a Hungarian Researcher of Faraway People.

My main project in Hungary was to rewrite a book I had started in the 1980's on the nature of art. I called it then "Towards a Natural

History of Art." My argument was that the basic nature of art was determined by the kind of society it was in, that, for example, the society decided whether the artist carved masks or painted with oil on canvas. I argued that artists are always capable of naturalistic representation but that naturalism is not always required of them. This book took many years to rewrite and was published in 2005 as *Thinking with Things*. In 1994 I was still struggling with the basics. Zsolt, whose book cover for *Equally Far From Everything* was a painting by a chimp, was interested in this approach to the definition of art. What was art and where was the line between non-art? The chimp painting looked like Modern Art but was it? My book took the global perspective on art in which I tried to answer some unfashionable questions. It was very difficult to formulate and I struggled a long time over it. Budapest with all its diverse intellectual currents was the ideal place to discuss it and write it.

My second project was to write a Pre-Columbian novel. I always imagined writing a novel about Teo and some quiet evenings in my home in Budapest I wrote about half of it. The story of *Daughter of the Pyramids* (2002) was about an American graduate student, Naomi, writing a novel about a dancing girl of Teo. The writer magically enters the past and becomes the girl, Marigold, and can't escape from her time. Naomi is anxious to get back into her real life in the US but gets involved in Marigold's adventures. Marigold is on her way to the Maya site of Tikal accompanied by her a lover, a mysterious Lord Smoke. Naomi figures out how to get back to her world about the time she reaches Tikal after many adventures. The question is: will she settle down in Mayaland or will she go back home to the US? Where is her true place in the world?

Naomi's problem of where to belong was of course my problem. While everyone asked if I would retire in Hungary I had mixed feelings. My initial reception had not been auspicious and not having gone to school there I did not have the contacts and associations that would have made for a large acquaintanceship. I was really there as an anthropologist trying to find out what my culture was like so that eventually I would know myself better. I came to Hungary to find some essential hungarianness. The more years I went the less possible that seemed to be as Hungary became more visibly globalized and the McDonalds and Pizza Huts were just the tip of the iceberg. An Ecuadorian musical group was in the habit of singing in the subway underpasses much enjoyed by the Budapest inhabitants. One weekend I encountered them in the artist colony/tourist village of Szentendre and heard passersby saying that it was too bad they could not have had a Hungarian group because the Ecuadorian group was "out of place." There are those who want Hungary to be cosmopolitan, global and modern and there are those who want it to be a Hungarian theme park and stop time. Mostly it's a little of both.

Kati Klimes once took me to a folk singing event in a forest clearing outside of Budapest (Pilisszentlászlo). Kati Szvorák and the Bekecs group were going to be singing for a group of Austrian ethnomusicologists. An "authentic" kettle-goulash (broth rather than stew) was cooking over a wood fire hung from a chain and tripod. Kati Szvorák was dressed in turquoise pants and a Valladolid t-shirt which proved her "authenticity" – any kind of peasant garb would have been theatrical and unnatural. Everyone in the Bekecs group looked like an intellectual with glasses. We ate the goulash which was very good. Kati sang and the Bekecs group played. The Austrians took notes on everything, made recordings and took pictures. Hungarianness was being constructed right then and there.

In the nineteenth century the German scholar Johann Herder predicted that the Hungarian language would go extinct in a short time because it was surrounded by Slavic languages. The theory and fear of extinction is in the back of the Hungarian mind. Cutting down Hungary at Versailles-Trianon was part of this dreaded extinction. Globalization is another part. Hungarians keep Hungary going by achieving something great, getting all the Nobel Prizes, the soccer World Cup in 1953 – anything that keeps Hungary in the news keeps it alive and far from extinct. We were all brought up to achieve for Hungary. Extinction is now actually threatened by demographics – women are not having enough babies and the population of ethnic Hungarians is shrinking. Many would like to see exiles and their children go back.

8
Hybrid Vigor

"Si del cielo te caen limones, aprende a hacer limonada."
If it rains lemons, learn to make lemonade.
Hispanic Proverb

In 2000 I married Richard Eaton who comes from Maine and has introduced me to yet another fascinating American region. He asked me to write this book. Six months after our wedding I was diagnosed with breast cancer and it took several years to get through the treatments and emotional trauma. The experience made me want to complete my various projects. While Richard loved Budapest it was obvious that we were going to spend less time there so I sold the apartment to my cousin Balint who lives in London but likes to visit. He made the apartment available for the family and we can and do go under his ownership. I had the furniture shipped to the US and shared it with my sister. Some of my favorite pieces are now in my New York apartment where I am taking them for granted. We now spend our summers in Maine where I learned to enjoy lobster.

Does this mean that my 1.5 generation pendulum has moved from Hungary to America again and after a time I can expect more turbulence and some sort of swing back or have I finally found some sort of a resting place in the middle? The "middle" would mean some sort of combination or hybridity, keeping some features of both and losing some. All my life I was too unwilling to lose anything to become a "hybrid," thinking of it more like a "mongrel mutt" than a "hybrid rose." I stayed away from hybrid periods in my research, too.

I used to hate the Colonial period in Latin America and never understood how some of my friends such as Cecelia were so enthusiastic about it. The Conquest in the sixteenth century was a grim affair of people with superior weapons bringing lethal diseases destroying whole civilizations. And if subliminally I equated the Spanish with the Russian on November 4, 1956, that was probably no surprise. But the Colonial period was even worse in my mind in the forced conversions, burnings at the stake, and the wholesale extirpations of native customs, art and thought until they disappeared almost entirely in a provincial Spanish/ native mish-mash. As far as I could see, Colonial art had neither the great Pre-Columbian tradition of Aztec and Maya sculpture or Teo painting nor the splendid Baroque art of France and Italy. It was pitiful.

A few years ago, Diana Fane, a colonial specialist and Columbia colleague asked me to teach a course with her on Colonial Art of the sixteenth century. While the idea was still somewhat foreign to me I agreed on the grounds that perhaps it was time to take a closer look and a chance to change my mind. I learned that my colleagues had found many more instances of native survivals in the Colonial period indicating that not everything had been immediately destroyed in the conquest. More-over, some native individuals did better in Colonial times than in earlier times and some were enthusiastic converts and even learned Latin. (My cynicism also recognized some that were opportunists who reminded me of people under communism.) Nevertheless, evidently some people survived and managed to deal successfully with the Colonial world. Intermarriage and sexual relations between the peoples were common from the beginning, giving rise within one generation to a racially mixed population. In many Latin American countries there was strict segrega-tion between people of Spanish and native or mixed blood, but in Mexico the hybrid called "mestizo" was recognized early as the bulk of the population. Most Mexicans accept their dual heritage and are proud of having last names like "Moctezuma."

My colleagues admire the artists of early Colonial Mexico for their exceptional creativity: the way natives combined Aztec with Spanish style in book illustration that is both harmonious and makes sense or the way they adapted Aztec featherwork from military dress to Spanish ec-clesiastical objects. They translated one culture into another. It takes a special creativity to transfer selectively one culture into another and Latin Americans have been doing it for centuries. Serge Gruzinsky, a colonial historian, has written a book entitled *The Mestizo Mind* in which he suggests that creativity is characteristic of the mestizo mind, and, as globalization proceeds in the rest of the world we are all acquiring mes-tizo minds.

The problems of globalization have been easier for me to deal with than colonialism. I had a dramatic encounter with it in Santa Fe in 1976 when I was looking at ruins with Adam. Just to pass the time I drifted into the Santa Fe Institute of American Indian Art museum where I seemed to be the only visitor. There were a lot of modernistic paintings with native titles like "Navajo Sunrise" but which were clearly influenced by Jackson Pollock and other modern paintings. Suddenly a man accosted me aggressively and said that I should not expect cute scenes of Indian rituals, that Indians are no longer painting such ethnic scenes for tourists, they want to be real artists doing modern art. "But you," he pointed a finger at me, "will not buy the modern paintings!" I escaped from him as soon as I could. I was not interested in the modern or the cute scenes, I was interested in ancient ruins. Nevertheless this event has stuck with me and I became aware of similar situations in other parts of the world. I was impressed by the anger of the man I believe to have been a curator and the desire to go mainstream and not to remain fully native forever. I then read other angry voices such as the Native American Jimmy Durham who accused Americans of wanting all their cultures that they have despoiled to be forever "virginal" and native and not allowed into the modern world. Rasheed Araeen, an Islamic Pakistani artist in London, has been one of the most explicit: "Somehow I began to feel that the context or history of modernism was not available to me, as I was reminded by other people of the relationship of my work to my Islamic tradition...you can no longer define, sir, classify or categorize me. I am no longer your bloody objects in the British Museum." The anger leapt off the page. Although at the time it must have been unconscious, but it must have reminded me of all the times my appropriateness to studying Pre-Columbian art was questioned with the implication that I should be studying Hungarian art or something similar. I understood the dilemma the ethnic artist faced in being forced to be ethnic by the system.

This interest led me to give a seminar a couple of times entitled "Modern Art Outside the West" in which the subject was the hybrid artist within the modern art world. As this subject turned out to have great interest to students and other professors, the faculty teaching Nonwestern art history joined me last year to teach a combined course (Multiple Modernities). By 2006 Nonwestern artists were no longer crying in the wilderness and some were in fact doing very well. Not only have many joined the mainstream, some have become stars of the art world. Curiously enough, however, the art world still demands some sign of their ethnicity in their work to be fully accepted as "exotics." For example, I came across the work of Yinka Shonibare in *Vogue* magazine at the hairdressers some years ago indicating significant popular success. Shonibare is of Nigerian origin and does installations that spoof Classical Western art, such as Fragonard's painting of "The Swing" at the Frick Museum. At first his work had no obvious African elements and so he was told to put something "African" in it. After all, he can't be European, so he must do something African. His European looking figures are now covered in a patchwork of "African" textiles. Ironically, while these textiles are commonly used in and identified with Africans, they are really of Dutch origins – so he has made fun of the issue. Shonibare has managed to create an African-Contemporary art in which the African and the European are completely blended. He is not alone; other artists in every country are appropriating Western tradition and blending it with their own in a great spurt of creativity and enjoyment.

I used to hate hybridity because it stopped the possibility of becoming a whole person in one direction or another. It meant living with loss. But in the meantime the world has caught up with my private loss and traditional societies are at an ebb everywhere, including Hungary. (I once saw a TV program showing how to make American-style salad for the housewife, to say nothing of the Tupperware party I attended in Budapest.) Gruzinsky may be right that we are all on the way to have "mestizo minds." I am acquiring sympathy for the Colonial period – what choices did they have after all and didn't they make the best of it? Hybridity may have its unplumbed joys.

I am also acquiring greater sympathy for my fellow Hungarian exiles and expatriates. I recognize that they deal with some of the same ambivalences that I have and I am not unique. Their Hungarian is archaic too and we frequent the concerts and dinners at the Hungarian consulate because we haven't blended into America society well enough and are nostalgic about a Hungary we can't blend into either. Being a 1.5 generation exile has had one silver lining for me – I always have a dual, even triple, perspective on issues differing from my American colleagues. Sometimes that is a curse, but mostly it's a blessing.

The year 2006 is the fiftieth anniversary of the Hungarian Revolution and many preparations are being made in the New York Hungarian community to celebrate it. Sadly, in Hungary the revolution has become a bone of contention for the current political parties. By an ugly process of polarization the revolution "belongs" to the Right, the conservatives and the exiles. The ruling Left in Hungary considers it to have been only a "middle class" revolution of "opportunists" whose interest in leaving the country was to make more money. Like the parties, ordinary Hungarians are divided on the issue. It is sad that a heroic uprising with so many dead and dispersed victims should be something that the country can't agree on fifty years later.

Illustrations

16.   Esther as Princess Kukachin in Eugene O'Neil's play *Marco Millions* at the Cambridge School of Weston, c. 1959

17.   Esther Pasztory at the ruins of Monte Alban, Mexico, c. 1965

18.   The ruins of Teotihuacan, Mexico, the Pyramid of the Sun in the background (1-600 AD)

Father László Miskolczy
with one of his buildings in the background, 1930's

Hotel Kékes, 1931

Dezső, Sándor, Ferenc, Lászlo Miskolczy as small children, c. 1901-02

From left to right: Ferenc, Sándor, Dezső Miskolczy seated, Lászlo standing as soldiers in World War I, c. 1917

Lászlo Miskolczy with architectural plan, probably New York

Wedding photo of Lászlo Miskolczy and Klara Konya, 1942

Grandmother Anna Nemes Konya with fan, probably, 1930's

Mother Klara Konya posing for modeling, 1941

Klara Miskolczy portrait photo, late 1940's

Klara Miskolczy with Kristina on the right and Esther on the left, c. 1947-1948

Esther's earliest existing photo

Esther practicing ballet in the living room of the Otto Herman Street apartment

School photo under communism. Esther stands in the center of the third row with the pigtails. Her friend Edda Ertl is on her right. They all wear the red kerchief of the pioneer uniform.

Bronze portrait head of Esther in a ponytail hairdo
by Béni Ferenczy, 1955

Drawing of Esther and Kristina by Béni Ferenczy, c. 1956.
Private Collection

Esther as Princess Kukachin in Eugene O'Neil's play *Marco Millions* at the Cambridge School of Weston, c. 1959

Esther Pasztory at the ruins of Monte Alban, Mexico, c. 1965

**The ruins of Teotihuacan, Mexico,
the Pyramid of the Sun in the background (1-600 AD)**